Indian

Notes for the Reader
This book uses both metric and imperial measurements. Follow the same units of
measurement throughout; do not mix metric and imperial. All spoon measurements are
level: teaspoons are assumed to be 5 ml, and tablespoons are assumed to be 15 ml.
Unless otherwise stated, milk is assumed to be full fat, eggs and individual vegetables
are medium, and pepper is freshly ground black pepper.

The times given are an approximate guide only. Preparation times differ according to
the techniques used by different people and the cooking times may also vary from
those given. Optional ingredients, variations or serving suggestions have not been
included in the calculations.

Recipes using raw or very lightly cooked eggs should be avoided by infants, the elderly,
pregnant women, convalescents and anyone suffering from an illness. Pregnant and
breastfeeding women are advised to avoid eating peanuts and peanut products.
Sufferers from nut allergies should be aware that some of the ready-made ingredients
used in the recipes in this book may contain nuts. Always check the packaging before
use.

Indian

introduction

Nowadays, supermarkets stock ingredients from across the world and city streets are lined with restaurants representing every imaginable country. In the West, Indian cooking is among the most popular of eastern cuisines, especially now that keen home cooks have discovered how easy it is to prepare authentic, tasty and nutritious Indian dishes. Perhaps the secrets of its popularity are its subtlety and extraordinary variety.

Given that the sub-continent is so huge, with an equally extensive history, it is hardly surprising that both its people and their diets are so diverse. Religious practices have had a profound influence – Hindus

don't eat beef, Muslims don't eat pork and Buddhists, among others, are vegetarian. Explorers, conquerors and colonizers have had an effect too, clearly seen in the rich-tasting dishes created for Moghul emperors or the use of vinegar in the curries of former

Portuguese territories, for example. Foreign ingredients are most often seen in the dishes of western India. Climate and topography also play their part and each region of the country has a unique style of cooking based on local  ingredients. In the north, dairy products such as yogurt and ghee (clarified butter) are featured, as well as nuts, while southern cooking is characterized by its use of coconuts, their oil and a variety of chillies. Eastern regions are famous for their fish dishes and mustard oil. Delhi is well known for tandoori cooking, Kashmir for its meat, especially lamb, Madras for its wealth of vegetarian dishes and Bengal for fine fish and tooth-achingly sweet desserts.

 However, the cuisines of all regions are united in the use of careful blends of spices, which are usually bought whole and ground as needed. These mixtures are subtle and aromatic but not invariably hot, although both fresh and dried chillies do feature in many dishes. With such a wide variety of choice, why not let Indian cuisine add a touch of spice to your culinary repertoire?

chicken

One of India's most popular meats, chicken is an excellent choice for curries and for cooking with subtle, aromatic spice blends. It can sometimes be rather bland so combining it with other flavoursome ingredients, from almonds, garlic and yogurt to onions, ginger, chillies, cumin and coriander, turns it into a real feast. Indian cooks will often choose the dark meat, which tends to have more flavour, but diced chicken breasts are ideal for stir-frying and can be substituted for thigh meat in other recipes according to taste.

Chicken is very versatile and is equally delicious roasted, braised, stir-fried or grilled on skewers – all in Indian-style. It is frequently marinated, often only briefly, or rubbed with a dry spice mixture before cooking to give the dish a real depth of flavour. Because of its texture, it works especially well with creamy mixtures, such as the perennially popular chicken korma from northern India. It is also great in spicier curries that range from the fragrant and mild to the fiery hot. Added to this, it goes well with a wide range of accompaniments – plain boiled rice, dhals and other lentil dishes, Indian breads and salads – so it's easy to add variety to the family menu.

chicken tikka masala

ingredients

SERVES 4–6

400 g/14 oz canned chopped
   tomatoes
300 ml/10 fl oz double cream
8 cooked tandoori chicken
   pieces (see page 32)
salt and pepper
fresh chopped coriander,
   to garnish
cooked basmati rice, to serve

tikka masala

30 g/1 oz ghee or 2 tbsp
   vegetable or groundnut oil
1 large garlic clove, finely
   chopped
1 fresh red chilli, deseeded
   and chopped
2 tsp ground cumin
2 tsp ground paprika
$1/2$ tsp salt
pepper

method

1 To make the tikka masala, melt the ghee in a large frying pan with a lid over a medium heat. Add the garlic and chilli and stir-fry for 1 minute. Stir in the cumin, paprika, salt and pepper to taste and continue stirring for about 30 seconds.

2 Stir the tomatoes and cream into the tikka masala. Reduce the heat to low and leave the sauce to simmer for about 10 minutes, stirring frequently, until it reduces and thickens.

3 Meanwhile, remove all the bones and any skin from the tandoori chicken pieces, then cut the meat into bite-sized pieces.

4 Adjust the seasoning of the sauce, if necessary. Add the chicken pieces to the pan, cover and leave to simmer for 3–5 minutes, until the chicken is heated through. Garnish with coriander and serve with cooked basmati rice.

chicken korma

ingredients

SERVES 4

1 chicken, weighing
	1.3 kg/3 lb
225 g/8 oz ghee or butter
3 onions, thinly sliced
1 garlic clove, crushed
2.5-cm/1-inch piece fresh
	ginger, grated
1 tsp mild chilli powder
1 tsp ground turmeric
1 tsp ground coriander
$1/2$ tsp ground cardamom
$1/2$ tsp ground cinnamon
$1/2$ tsp salt
1 tbsp gram flour
125 ml/4 fl oz milk
500 ml/18 fl oz double cream
fresh coriander leaves,
	to garnish
freshly cooked rice, to serve

method

1 Put the chicken into a large saucepan, cover with water and bring to the boil. Reduce the heat, cover and simmer for 30 minutes. Remove from the heat, lift out the chicken and set aside to cool. Reserve 125 ml/4 fl oz of the cooking liquid. Remove and discard the skin and bones. Cut the flesh into bite-sized pieces.

2 Heat the ghee in a large saucepan over a medium heat. Add the onions and garlic and cook, stirring, for 3 minutes, or until softened. Add the ginger, chilli powder, turmeric, ground coriander, cardamom, cinnamon and salt and cook for a further 5 minutes. Add the chicken and the reserved cooking liquid. Cook for 2 minutes.

3 Blend the flour with a little of the milk and add to the pan, then stir in the remaining milk. Bring to the boil, stirring, then reduce the heat, cover and simmer for 25 minutes. Stir in the cream, cover and simmer for a further 15 minutes.

4 Garnish with coriander leaves and serve with freshly cooked rice.

kashmiri chicken

ingredients

SERVES 4–6

seeds from 8 green
    cardamom pods
$^{1}/_{2}$ tsp coriander seeds
$^{1}/_{2}$ tsp cumin seeds
1 cinnamon stick
8 black peppercorns
6 cloves
1 tbsp hot water
$^{1}/_{2}$ tsp saffron threads
40 g/1$^{1}/_{2}$ oz ghee or 3 tbsp
    vegetable or groundnut oil
1 large onion, finely chopped
2 tbsp garlic and ginger paste
250 ml/9 fl oz natural yogurt
8 skinless, boneless chicken
    thighs, sliced
3 tbsp ground almonds
55 g/2 oz blanched pistachio
    nuts, finely chopped
2 tbsp chopped fresh
    coriander
2 tbsp chopped fresh mint
salt
toasted flaked almonds,
    to garnish
Indian bread, to serve

method

1 Dry-roast the cardamom seeds in a frying pan over a medium–low heat, stirring constantly, until you can smell the aroma. Repeat with the coriander and cumin seeds, cinnamon, peppercorns and cloves. Put all the spices, except the cinnamon stick, in a spice grinder and grind to a powder.

2 Put the hot water and saffron threads in a small bowl and set aside.

3 Melt the ghee in a flameproof casserole. Add the onion and cook, stirring occasionally, over a medium–high heat for 5–8 minutes, until golden brown. Add the garlic and ginger paste and continue stirring for 2 minutes.

4 Stir in the ground spices and the cinnamon stick. Remove from the heat and mix in the yogurt, a small amount at a time, stirring vigorously with each addition, then return to the heat and continue stirring for 2–3 minutes, until the ghee separates. Add the chicken pieces.

5 Bring to the boil, stirring constantly, then reduce the heat to low, cover and simmer for 20 minutes, stirring occasionally.

6 Stir in the ground almonds, pistachios, saffron with its soaking liquid, half the coriander, all the mint and salt to taste. Re-cover the pan and continue simmering for about 5 minutes, until the chicken is tender and the sauce is thickened. Sprinkle with the remaining coriander and the flaked almonds and serve with Indian bread.

chicken jalfrezi

ingredients

SERVES 4–6

55 g/2 oz ghee or 4 tbsp
    vegetable or groundnut oil
8 skinless, boneless chicken
    thighs, sliced
1 large onion, chopped
2 tbsp garlic and ginger paste
2 green peppers, cored,
    deseeded and chopped
1 large fresh green chilli,
    deseeded and finely
    chopped
1 tsp ground cumin
1 tsp ground coriander
$^{1}/_{4}$–$^{1}/_{2}$ tsp chilli powder
$^{1}/_{2}$ tsp ground turmeric
$^{1}/_{4}$ tsp salt
400 g/14 oz canned chopped
    tomatoes
125 ml/4 fl oz water
chopped fresh coriander,
    to garnish

method

1 Melt half the ghee in a wok or large frying pan over a medium–high heat. Add the chicken pieces and stir around for 5 minutes, until browned but not necessarily cooked through, then remove from the pan with a slotted spoon and set aside.

2 Melt the remaining ghee in the pan. Add the onion and fry, stirring frequently, for 5–8 minutes, until golden brown. Stir in the garlic and ginger paste and continue frying for 2 minutes, stirring frequently.

3 Add the peppers to the pan and stir around for 2 minutes.

4 Stir in the chilli, cumin, coriander, chilli powder, turmeric and salt. Add the tomatoes with their juice and the water and bring to the boil.

5 Reduce the heat to low, add the chicken and leave it to simmer, uncovered, for 10 minutes, stirring frequently, until the peppers are tender, the chicken is cooked through and the juices run clear if you pierce a few pieces with the tip of a knife. Sprinkle with the coriander.

balti chicken

ingredients

SERVES 6

3 tbsp ghee or vegetable oil

2 large onions, sliced

3 tomatoes, sliced

$1/2$ tsp kalonji seeds

4 black peppercorns

2 green cardamom pods

1 cinnamon stick

1 tsp chilli powder

1 tsp garam masala

2 tsp garlic and ginger paste

700 g/1 lb 9 oz skinless,
    boneless chicken breasts
    or thighs, diced

2 tbsp natural yogurt

2 tbsp chopped fresh
    coriander, plus extra
    sprigs to garnish

2 fresh green chillies,
    deseeded and finely
    chopped

2 tbsp lime juice

salt

method

1 Heat the ghee in a large heavy-based frying pan. Add the onions and cook over a low heat, stirring occasionally, for 10 minutes, or until golden. Add the tomatoes, kalonji seeds, peppercorns, cardamom pods, cinnamon stick, chilli powder, garam masala, and garlic and ginger paste, and season to taste with salt. Cook, stirring constantly, for 5 minutes.

2 Add the chicken and cook, stirring constantly, for 5 minutes, or until well coated in the spice paste. Stir in the yogurt. Cover and simmer, stirring occasionally, for 10 minutes.

3 Stir in the chopped coriander, chillies and lime juice. Transfer to a warmed serving dish, garnish with coriander sprigs and serve immediately.

butter chicken

ingredients

SERVES 4–6

1 onion, chopped

1$^1/_2$ tbsp garlic and ginger
   paste

400 g/14 oz canned chopped
   tomatoes

$^1/_4$–$^1/_2$ tsp chilli powder

pinch of sugar

30 g/1 oz ghee or 2 tbsp
   vegetable or groundnut oil

125 ml/4 fl oz water

1 tbsp tomato purée

40 g/1$^1/_2$ oz butter, cut into
   small pieces

$^1/_2$ tsp garam masala

$^1/_2$ tsp ground cumin

$^1/_2$ tsp ground coriander

8 cooked tandoori chicken
   pieces (see page 32)

4 tbsp double cream

salt and pepper

chopped cashew nuts and
   fresh coriander sprigs,
   to garnish

method

1 Put the onion and garlic and ginger paste in a food processor, blender or spice grinder and whizz together until a paste forms. Add the tomatoes, chilli powder, sugar and a pinch of salt and whizz again until blended.

2 Melt the ghee in a wok or large frying pan over a medium–high heat. Add the tomato mixture and water and stir in the tomato pureé.

3 Bring the mixture to the boil, stirring, then reduce the heat to very low and simmer for 5 minutes, stirring occasionally, until the sauce thickens.

4 Stir in half the butter, the garam masala, cumin and coriander. Add the chicken pieces and stir around until they are well coated. Simmer for a further 10 minutes, or until the chicken is hot. Taste and adjust the seasoning, if necessary.

5 Lightly beat the cream in a small bowl and stir in several tablespoons of the hot sauce, beating constantly. Stir the cream mixture into the tomato sauce, then add the remaining butter and stir until it melts. Garnish with the chopped cashew nuts and coriander sprigs and serve straight from the pan.

wok-cooked chicken in tomato & fenugreek sauce

ingredients

SERVES 4

700 g/1 lb 9 oz skinless,
  boneless chicken thighs,
  cut into 2.5-cm/1-inch
  cubes
juice of 1 lime
1 tsp salt, or to taste
4 tbsp sunflower or olive oil
1 large onion, finely chopped
2 tsp ginger purée
2 tsp garlic purée
$1/2$ tsp ground turmeric
$1/2$–1 tsp chilli powder
1 tbsp ground coriander
425 g/15 oz canned chopped
  tomatoes
125 ml/4 fl oz warm water
1 tbsp dried fenugreek leaves
$1/2$ tsp garam masala
2 tbsp chopped fresh
  coriander leaves
2–4 fresh green chillies
Indian bread, to serve

method

1 Place the chicken in a non-metallic bowl and rub in the lime juice and salt. Cover and set aside for 30 minutes.

2 Heat the oil in a wok or heavy-based frying pan over a medium–high heat. Add the onion and stir-fry for 7–8 minutes, until it begins to colour.

3 Add the ginger and garlic purées and continue to stir-fry for about a minute. Add the turmeric, chilli powder and ground coriander, then reduce the heat slightly and cook the spices for 25–30 seconds. Add half the tomatoes, stir-fry for 3–4 minutes and add the remaining tomatoes. Continue to cook, stirring, until the tomato juice has evaporated and the oil separates from the spice paste and floats on the surface.

4 Add the chicken and increase the heat to high. Stir-fry for 4–5 minutes, then add the warm water, reduce the heat to medium–low and cook for 8–10 minutes, or until the sauce has thickened and the chicken is tender.

5 Add the fenugreek leaves, garam masala, half the coriander leaves and the chillies. Cook for 1–2 minutes, remove from the heat and transfer to a serving plate. Garnish with the remaining coriander and serve with Indian bread.

chicken with stir-fried spices

ingredients

SERVES 4

700 g/1 lb 9 oz skinless,
 boneless chicken breasts
 or thighs

juice of $\frac{1}{2}$ lemon

1 tsp salt, or to taste

5 tbsp sunflower or olive oil

1 large onion, finely chopped

2 tsp garlic purée

2 tsp ginger purée

$\frac{1}{2}$ tsp ground turmeric

1 tsp ground cumin

2 tsp ground coriander

$\frac{1}{2}$–1 tsp chilli powder

150 g/5$\frac{1}{2}$ oz canned chopped
 tomatoes

150 ml/5 fl oz warm water

1 large garlic clove, finely
 chopped

1 small or $\frac{1}{2}$ large red
 pepper, deseeded and cut
 into 2.5-cm/1-inch pieces

1 small or $\frac{1}{2}$ large green
 pepper, deseeded and cut
 into 2.5-cm/1-inch pieces

1 tsp garam masala

Indian bread, to serve

method

1 Cut the chicken into 2.5-cm/1-inch cubes and put in a non-metallic bowl. Add the lemon juice and half the salt and rub well into the chicken. Cover and leave to marinate in the refrigerator for 20 minutes.

2 Heat 4 tablespoons of the oil in a medium heavy-based saucepan over a medium heat. Add the onion and cook, stirring frequently, for 8–9 minutes, until lightly browned. Add the garlic and ginger pureés and cook, stirring, for 3 minutes. Add the turmeric, cumin, coriander and chilli powder and cook, stirring, for 1 minute. Add the tomatoes and their juice and cook for 2–3 minutes, stirring frequently, until the oil separates from the spice paste.

3 Add the marinated chicken, increase the heat slightly and cook, stirring, until it changes colour. Add the warm water and bring to the boil. Reduce the heat, cover and simmer for 25 minutes.

4 Heat the remaining 1 tablespoon of oil in a small saucepan or frying pan over a low heat. Add the garlic and cook, stirring frequently, until browned. Add the peppers, increase the heat to medium and stir-fry for 2 minutes, then stir in the garam masala. Fold the pepper mixture into the curry. Remove from the heat and serve immediately with Indian bread.

cumin-scented chicken

ingredients

SERVES 4

700 g/1 lb 9 oz boneless
   chicken thighs or breasts,
   cut into 5-cm/2-inch
   pieces
juice of 1 lime
1 tsp salt, or to taste
3 tbsp sunflower or olive oil
1 tsp cumin seeds
2.5-cm/1-inch piece
   cinnamon stick
5 green cardamom pods,
   bruised
4 cloves
1 large onion, finely chopped
2 tsp garlic purée
2 tsp ginger purée
$1/2$ tsp ground turmeric
2 tsp ground cumin
$1/2$ tsp chilli powder
225 g/8 oz canned chopped
   tomatoes
1 tbsp tomato purée
$1/2$ tsp sugar
225 ml/8 fl oz warm water
$1/2$ tsp garam masala
2 tbsp chopped fresh
   coriander leaves, plus
   extra sprigs to garnish
Indian bread, to serve

method

1 Put the chicken in a non-metallic bowl and rub in the lime juice and salt. Cover and set aside for 30 minutes.

2 Heat the oil in a medium saucepan over a low heat and add the cumin seeds, cinnamon, cardamom and cloves. Let them sizzle for 25–30 seconds, then add the onion. Cook, stirring regularly, for 5 minutes, or until the onion is soft.

3 Add the garlic and ginger purées and cook for about a minute, then add the turmeric, ground cumin and chilli powder. Add the tomatoes, tomato purée and sugar. Cook over a medium heat, stirring regularly, until the tomatoes reach a paste-like consistency and the oil separates from the paste. Sprinkle over a little water if the mixture sticks to the pan.

4 Add the chicken and increase the heat to medium–high. Stir until the chicken changes colour, then pour in the warm water. Bring to the boil, reduce the heat to medium–low and cook for 12–15 minutes, or until the sauce has thickened and the chicken is tender.

5 Stir in the garam masala and chopped coriander. Transfer to a serving dish and garnish with coriander sprigs. Serve with Indian bread.

chicken in green chilli, mint & coriander sauce

ingredients

SERVES 4

25 g/1 oz coriander leaves
   and stalks, roughly chopped
25 g/1 oz fresh spinach,
   roughly chopped
2.5-cm/1-inch piece fresh
   ginger, roughly chopped
3 garlic cloves, roughly
   chopped
2–3 fresh green chillies,
   roughly chopped
15 g/^{1}/$_{2}$ oz fresh mint leaves
1^{1}/$_{2}$ tbsp lemon juice
^{1}/$_{2}$ tsp salt, or to taste
85 g/3 oz thick set natural
   yogurt
4 tbsp sunflower or olive oil
1 large onion, finely chopped
700 g/1 lb 9 oz skinless
   chicken thighs or breasts,
   cut into 2.5-cm/1-inch
   cubes
1 tsp ground turmeric
^{1}/$_{2}$ tsp sugar
1 small tomato, deseeded
   and cut into julienne
   strips, to garnish
cooked basmati rice, to serve

method

1 Place the coriander, spinach, ginger, garlic, chillies, mint, lemon juice and the ^{1}/$_{2}$ teaspoon of salt in a food processor or blender and process to a smooth purée. Add a little water, if necessary, to facilitate blade movement in a blender. Remove and set aside.

2 Whisk the yogurt until smooth (this is important as the yogurt will curdle otherwise) and set aside.

3 Heat the oil in a medium saucepan and cook the onion for 5–6 minutes, stirring regularly, until soft.

4 Add the chicken and stir-fry over a medium–high heat for 2–3 minutes, until the meat turns opaque. Add the turmeric and sugar, with a little more salt if necessary, and stir-fry for a further 2 minutes, then reduce the heat to medium and add half the yogurt. Cook for 1 minute and add the remaining yogurt, then continue cooking over a medium heat until the yogurt resembles a thick batter and the oil is visible.

5 Add the puréed ingredients and cook for 4–5 minutes, stirring constantly. Remove from the heat and garnish with the strips of tomato. Serve with cooked basmati rice.

quick chicken curry with mushrooms & beans

ingredients

SERVES 4

55 g/2 oz ghee or 4 tbsp
   vegetable or groundnut oil
8 skinless, boneless chicken
   thighs, sliced
1 small onion, chopped
2 large garlic cloves, crushed
100 g/3^1/$_2$ oz green beans,
   trimmed and chopped
100 g/3^1/$_2$ oz mushrooms,
   thickly sliced
2 tbsp milk
salt and pepper
fresh coriander sprigs,
   to garnish
cooked basmati rice, to serve

curry paste

2 tsp garam masala
1 tsp mild, medium or hot
   curry powder, to taste
1 tbsp water

method

1 To make the curry paste, put the garam masala and curry powder in a bowl and stir in the water, then set aside.

2 Melt half the ghee in a large heavy-based saucepan or frying pan with a tight-fitting lid over a medium–high heat. Add the chicken and curry paste and stir around for 5 minutes.

3 Add the onion, garlic and green beans and continue cooking for a further 5 minutes, until the chicken is cooked through and the juices run clear.

4 Add the remaining ghee and mushrooms and, when the ghee melts, stir in the milk. Season to taste with salt and pepper. Reduce the heat to low, cover and simmer for 10 minutes, stirring occasionally. Garnish with coriander sprigs and serve with cooked basmati rice.

chicken biryani

ingredients

SERVES 8

small piece fresh ginger

1¹/₂ tsp crushed garlic

1 tbsp garam masala

1 tsp chilli powder

2 tsp salt

5 green cardamom pods,
    bruised

300 ml/10 fl oz natural yogurt

1 chicken, weighing 1.5 kg/
    3 lb 5 oz

150 ml/5 fl oz milk

1¹/₂ tsp saffron strands

6 tbsp ghee

2 onions, sliced

450 g/1 lb basmati rice

2 cinnamon sticks

4 fresh green chillies

2 tbsp coriander leaves

4 tbsp lemon juice

method

1 Finely chop the ginger, then put it in a bowl with the garlic, garam masala, chilli powder, half the salt, and the cardamom pods. Add the yogurt. Skin the chicken, cut into 8 pieces, then add the pieces to the yoghurt mixture and mix well. Cover and leave to marinate in the refrigerator for 3 hours.

2 Pour the milk into a small saucepan, bring to the boil, then sprinkle over the saffron and reserve.

3 Heat the ghee in a saucepan. Add the onions and fry until golden. Transfer half of the onions and ghee to a bowl and reserve.

4 Place the rice and cinnamon sticks in a saucepan of water. Bring the rice to the boil and simmer for 4–5 minutes, then remove from the heat. Drain and place in a bowl. Mix with the remaining salt.

5 Chop the chillies and coriander leaves and reserve. Add the chicken mixture to the saucepan containing the onions. Add half each of the chopped green chillies, lemon juice, coriander and saffron milk. Add the rice, then the rest of the ingredients, including the reserved onions and ghee. Cover tightly. Cook over a low heat for 1 hour. Check that the meat is cooked through; if it is not cooked, return to the heat and cook for a further 15 minutes. Mix well before serving.

tandoori chicken

ingredients

SERVES 4

4 chicken pieces, about
225 g/8 oz each, skinned

juice of 1/2 lemon

1/2 tsp salt, or to taste

85 g/3 oz whole milk natural
yogurt, strained, or Greek-
style yogurt

3 tbsp double cream

1 tbsp gram flour

1 tbsp garlic purée

1 tbsp ginger purée

1/2–1 tsp chilli powder

1 tsp ground coriander

1/2 tsp ground cumin

1/2 tsp garam masala

1/2 tsp ground turmeric

2 tbsp vegetable oil,
for brushing

3 tbsp melted butter or olive oil

salad, to serve

lemon wedges, to garnish

method

1 Make 2–3 small incisions in each chicken piece and place in a large non-metallic bowl. Rub in the lemon juice and salt, cover and chill in the refrigerator for 20 minutes.

2 Meanwhile, put the yogurt in a separate bowl and add the cream and gram flour. Beat with a fork until well blended and smooth. Add all the remaining ingredients, except the oil and melted butter, and mix thoroughly. Pour the over the chicken and rub in well. Cover and chill in the refrigerator for 4–6 hours, or overnight. Return to room temperature before cooking.

3 Preheat the grill to high. Line a grill pan with foil and brush the rack with oil. Using tongs, lift the chicken pieces out of the marinade and put on the prepared rack, reserving the remaining marinade. Cook the chicken under the preheated grill for 4 minutes, then turn over and cook for a further 4 minutes. Baste the chicken generously with the reserved marinade and cook for a further 2 minutes on each side.

4 Brush the chicken with the melted butter and cook for 5–6 minutes, or until charred in patches. Turn over and baste with the remaining marinade. Cook for a further 5–6 minutes, or until charred as before and the juices run clear when a skewer is inserted into the thickest part of the meat.

5 Transfer the chicken to a dish. Serve with salad and garnish with lemon wedges.

silky chicken kebabs

ingredients

SERVES 8

55 g/2 oz raw cashew nuts

2 tbsp single cream

1 egg

450 g/1 lb skinless, boneless
chicken breasts, roughly
chopped

$1/2$ tsp salt, or to taste

2 tsp garlic purée

2 tsp ginger purée

2 fresh green chillies, roughly
chopped (deseeded
if you like)

15 g/$1/2$ oz fresh coriander,
including the tender
stalks, roughly chopped

1 tsp garam masala

vegetable oil, for brushing

25 g/1 oz butter, melted

chutney, to serve

method

1 Put the cashew nuts in a heatproof bowl, cover with boiling water and leave to soak for 20 minutes. Drain and put in a food processor. Add the cream and egg and process the ingredients to a coarse mixture.

2 Add all the remaining ingredients, except the oil and melted butter, and process until smooth. Transfer to a bowl, cover and chill in the refrigerator for 30 minutes.

3 Preheat the grill to high. Brush the rack and 8 metal or pre-soaked wooden skewers lightly with oil. Have a bowl of cold water ready.

4 Divide the chilled mixture into 8 equal-sized portions. Dip your hands into the bowl of cold water – this will stop the mixture sticking to your fingers when you are moulding it onto the skewers. Carefully mould each portion onto a skewer, forming it into a 15-cm/6-inch sausage shape. Arrange the kebabs on the prepared rack and cook under the preheated grill for 4 minutes. Brush with half the melted butter and cook for a further minute. Turn over and cook for 3 minutes. Baste with the remaining melted butter and cook for a further 2 minutes.

5 Remove from the heat and leave the kebabs to rest for 5 minutes before sliding them off the skewers with a knife. Serve with chutney.

creamy chicken tikka

ingredients

SERVES 4

700 g/1 lb 9 oz skinless,
    boneless chicken breasts,
    cut into 2.5-cm/1-inch
    cubes
2 tbsp lemon juice
$^1/_2$ tsp salt, or to taste
125 g/4$^1/_2$ oz whole milk
    natural yogurt, strained,
    or Greek-style yogurt
3 tbsp double cream
25 g/1 oz mild Cheddar
    cheese, grated
1 tbsp garlic purée
1 tbsp ginger purée
$^1/_2$–1 tsp chilli powder
$^1/_2$ tsp ground turmeric
$^1/_2$ tsp granulated sugar
1 tbsp gram flour, sifted
1 tsp garam masala
2 tbsp sunflower or olive oil,
    plus 2 tbsp for brushing
3 tbsp melted butter or olive oil
salad and chutney, to serve

method

1 Put the chicken in a non-metallic bowl and add the lemon juice and salt. Rub well into the chicken. Cover and leave to marinate in the refrigerator for 20–30 minutes.

2 Put the yogurt in a separate non-metallic bowl and beat with a fork until smooth. Add all the remaining ingredients, except the melted butter. Beat well until the ingredients are fully incorporated. Add the chicken and mix thoroughly until fully coated with the marinade. Cover and leave to marinate in the refrigerator for 4–6 hours, or overnight. Return to room temperature before cooking.

3 Preheat the grill to high. Brush 6 metal skewers generously with the remaining 2 tablespoons of oil and thread on the chicken cubes. Brush over any remaining marinade. Place the prepared skewers in a grill pan and grill about 7.5 cm/ 3 inches below the heat source for 4–5 minutes. Brush generously with the melted butter and cook for a further 1–2 minutes. Turn over and cook for 3–4 minutes, basting frequently with the remaining melted butter.

4 Balance the skewers over a large saucepan or frying pan and leave to rest for 5–6 minutes before sliding the chicken cubes off the skewers with a knife. Serve with salad and chutney.

meat

Because India was historically a poor country, meat dishes did not feature in the everyday menus of ordinary people but were usually served only on special occasions or in the homes of the rich. As a result, they are particularly succulent, thoughtfully spiced and exceptionally delicious.

Mutton or lamb is far and away the most commonly eaten meat in India and it is prepared in a wide variety of ways in the different regions of this vast country – marinated and served in a fragrant yogurt sauce, minced and shaped into meatballs or koftas, curried with a variety of vegetables or delicately spiced and grilled on skewers. Indian ways with lamb chops are so different from those in western kitchens that, if you haven't already tried them, these recipes simply must be explored.

Pork is the second most popular meat and recipes often show the culinary influence of foreigners. For example, the fiery hot vindaloo with its distinctive and unique flavouring of spices and vinegar originated in what was once Portuguese Goa.

Beef is less commonly used in India but features in Muslim cooking with many of the dishes originating in the south of the country. Perhaps the most famous of these is the robust Madras curry.

lamb rogan josh

ingredients

SERVES 4

350 ml/12 fl oz natural yogurt

1/2 tsp ground asafoetida,
    dissolved in 2 tbsp water

700 g/1 lb 9 oz boneless leg
    of lamb, trimmed and cut
    into 5-cm/2-inch cubes

2 tomatoes, deseeded and
    chopped

1 onion, chopped

25 g/1 oz ghee or 2 tbsp
    vegetable or groundnut oil

1 1/2 tbsp garlic and ginger
    paste

2 tbsp tomato purée

2 bay leaves

1 tbsp ground coriander

1/4–1 tsp chilli powder, ideally
    Kashmiri chilli powder

1/2 tsp ground turmeric

1 tsp salt

1/2 tsp garam masala

method

1 Put the yogurt in a large bowl and stir in the dissolved asafoetida. Add the lamb and use your hands to rub in all the marinade, then set aside for 30 minutes.

2 Meanwhile, put the tomatoes and onion in a blender and process until blended.

3 Melt the ghee in a flameproof casserole or large frying pan with a tight-fitting lid. Add the garlic and ginger paste and stir around until the aromas are released. Stir in the tomato mixture, tomato purée, bay leaves, coriander, chilli powder and turmeric, reduce the heat to low and simmer, stirring occasionally, for 5–8 minutes.

4 Add the lamb and salt with any leftover marinade and stir around for 2 minutes. Cover, reduce the heat to low and simmer, stirring occasionally, for 30 minutes. The lamb should give off enough moisture to prevent it from catching on the base of the pan, but if the sauce looks too dry, stir in a little water.

5 Sprinkle with the garam masala, re-cover the pan and continue simmering for 15–20 minutes, until the lamb is tender. Serve immediately.

peshawar-style lamb curry

ingredients

SERVES 4

4 tbsp sunflower or olive oil

2.5-cm/1-inch piece
cinnamon stick

5 green cardamom pods,
bruised

5 cloves

2 bay leaves

700 g/1 lb 9 oz boneless leg
of lamb, cut into 2.5-cm/
1-inch cubes

1 large onion, finely chopped

2 tsp ginger purée

2 tsp garlic purée

1 tbsp tomato purée

1 tsp ground turmeric

1 tsp ground coriander

1 tsp ground cumin

125 g/4$^{1}/_{2}$ oz thick set natural
yogurt

2 tsp gram flour or cornflour

$^{1}/_{2}$–1 tsp chilli powder

150 ml/5 fl oz warm water

1 tbsp chopped fresh mint
leaves

2 tbsp chopped fresh
coriander leaves

Indian bread, to serve

method

1 In a medium saucepan, heat the oil over a low heat and add the cinnamon, cardamom, cloves and bay leaves. Let them sizzle for 25–30 seconds, then add the meat, increase the heat to medium–high and cook until the meat begins to brown and all the natural juices have evaporated.

2 Add the onion and ginger and garlic purées, cook for 5–6 minutes, stirring regularly, then add the tomato purée, turmeric, ground coriander and cumin. Continue to cook for 3–4 minutes.

3 Whisk together the yogurt, gram flour and chilli powder and add to the meat. Reduce the heat to low, add the warm water, cover and simmer, stirring to ensure that the sauce does not stick to the base of the pan, for 45–50 minutes, or until the meat is tender. Simmer uncovered, if necessary, to thicken the sauce to a desired consistency.

4 Stir in the fresh mint and coriander, remove from the heat and serve with Indian bread.

lamb dopiaza

ingredients

SERVES 4

4 onions, sliced into rings

3 garlic cloves, roughly
    chopped

2.5-cm/1-inch piece fresh
    ginger, grated

1 tsp ground coriander

1 tsp ground cumin

1 tsp chilli powder

1/2 tsp ground turmeric

1 tsp ground cinnamon

1 tsp garam masala

4 tbsp water

5 tbsp ghee or vegetable oil

600 g/1 lb 5 oz boneless
    lamb, cut into bite-sized
    chunks

6 tbsp natural yogurt

salt and pepper

fresh coriander leaves,
    to garnish

cooked basmati rice, to serve

method

1 Put half of the onions into a food processor with the garlic, ginger, ground coriander, cumin, chilli powder, turmeric, cinnamon and garam masala. Add the water and process to a paste.

2 Heat 4 tablespoons of the ghee in a saucepan over a medium heat. Add the remaining onions and cook, stirring, for 3 minutes. Remove from the heat. Lift out the onions with a slotted spoon and set aside. Heat the remaining ghee in the pan over a high heat, add the lamb and cook, stirring, for 5 minutes. Lift out the meat and drain on kitchen paper.

3 Add the onion paste to the pan and cook over a medium heat, stirring, until the oil separates. Stir in the yogurt, season to taste with salt and pepper, return the lamb to the pan and stir well.

4 Bring the mixture gently to the boil, reduce the heat, cover and simmer for 25 minutes. Stir in the reserved onion rings and cook for a further 5 minutes. Remove from the heat, and garnish with coriander leaves. Serve immediately with cooked basmati rice.

lamb & spinach curry

ingredients

SERVES 2–4

300 ml/10 fl oz vegetable oil

2 onions, sliced

2 tbsp chopped fresh
    coriander

2 fresh green chillies, chopped

$1^1/_2$ tsp finely chopped fresh
    ginger

$1^1/_2$ tsp crushed garlic

1 tsp chilli powder

$^1/_2$ tsp ground turmeric

450 g/1 lb lean lamb, cut into
    bite-sized chunks

1 tsp salt

1 kg/2 lb 4 oz fresh spinach,
    trimmed, washed and
    chopped

700 ml/1$^1/_4$ pints water

finely chopped fresh red
    chilli, to garnish

method

1 Heat the oil in a large heavy-based frying pan. Add the onions and cook until golden.

2 Add the fresh coriander and green chillies to the frying pan and stir-fry for 3–5 minutes. Reduce the heat and add the ginger, garlic, chilli powder and turmeric, stirring well.

3 Add the lamb to the frying pan and stir-fry for a further 5 minutes. Add the salt and the spinach and cook, stirring occasionally with a wooden spoon, for a further 3–5 minutes.

4 Add the water, stirring, and cook over a low heat, covered, for 45 minutes. Remove the lid and check the meat. If it is not tender, turn the meat over, increase the heat and cook, uncovered, until the surplus water has been absorbed. Stir-fry the mixture for a further 5–7 minutes.

5 Transfer the lamb and spinach mixture to a serving dish and garnish with chopped red chilli. Serve hot.

lamb with cauliflower

ingredients

SERVES 4

30 g/1 oz ghee or 2 tbsp
    vegetable or groundnut oil
1 onion, chopped
$^1/_2$ tbsp garlic and ginger
    paste
1 tbsp cumin seeds
2 tsp mild, medium or hot
    curry paste, to taste
1 head cauliflower, broken
    into small florets
400 g/14 oz canned chopped
    tomatoes
125 ml/4 fl oz vegetable stock
    or water
700 g/1 lb 9 oz lamb neck
    fillet, trimmed and cut into
    5-mm/$^1/_4$-inch slices
lemon juice, to taste
salt and pepper
chopped fresh mint,
    to garnish

method

1 Melt the ghee in a wok or large frying pan over a medium–high heat. Add the onion and garlic and ginger paste and fry, stirring frequently, for 5–8 minutes, until the onion is lightly browned.

2 Add the cumin seeds and curry paste and stir around for about 1 minute. Add the cauliflower and continue stirring for a further minute.

3 Add the tomatoes with their juice, the stock and salt and pepper to taste. Bring to the boil, then reduce the heat and simmer for 10 minutes, stirring occasionally, until the sauce is reduced and the tomatoes break down.

4 Add the lamb and continue simmering, stirring occasionally, for 10 minutes, or until it is tender and just pink in the centre. Add lemon juice to taste and adjust the seasoning, if necessary. Serve garnished with a generous amount of mint.

lamb pasanda

ingredients

SERVES 4–6

600 g/1 lb 5 oz boneless
    shoulder or leg of lamb

2 tbsp garlic and ginger paste

55 g/2 oz ghee or 4 tbsp
    vegetable or groundnut oil

3 large onions, chopped

1 fresh green chilli, deseeded
    and chopped

2 green cardamom pods,
    bruised

1 cinnamon stick, broken
    in half

2 tsp ground coriander

1 tsp ground cumin

1 tsp ground turmeric

250 ml/9 fl oz water

150 ml/5 fl oz double cream

4 tbsp ground almonds

1 1/2 tsp salt

1 tsp garam masala

paprika and toasted flaked
    almonds, to garnish

method

1 Cut the meat into thin slices, then place the slices between clingfilm and pound with a meat mallet to make them even thinner. Put the lamb slices in a bowl, add the garlic and ginger paste and rub well into the lamb. Cover and leave to marinate in the refrigerator for 2 hours.

2 Melt the ghee in a large frying pan over a medium–high heat. Add the onions and chilli and cook, stirring frequently, for 5–8 minutes, until golden brown.

3 Stir in the cardamom pods, cinnamon stick, ground coriander, cumin and turmeric and continue stirring for 2 minutes, or until the spices are aromatic.

4 Add the meat to the pan and cook, stirring occasionally, for about 5 minutes, until it is brown on all sides and the fat begins to separate. Stir in the water and bring to the boil, still stirring. Reduce the heat to its lowest setting, cover the pan tightly and simmer for 40 minutes, or until the meat is tender.

5 Mix the cream and ground almonds together in a bowl. Beat in 6 tablespoons of the hot cooking liquid from the pan, then gradually beat this mixture back into the pan. Stir in the salt and garam masala. Continue to simmer for a further 5 minutes, uncovered, stirring occasionally.

6 Garnish with a sprinkling of paprika and flaked almonds and serve.

meatballs in creamy cashew nut sauce

ingredients

SERVES 4

450 g/1 lb fresh lean lamb
  mince
1 tbsp thick set natural yogurt
1 egg, beaten
$1/2$ tsp ground cardamom
$1/2$ tsp ground nutmeg
$1/2$ tsp pepper
$1/2$ tsp dried mint
$1/2$ tsp salt, or to taste
300 ml/10 fl oz water
2.5-cm/1-inch piece
  cinnamon stick
5 green cardamom pods
5 cloves
2 bay leaves
3 tbsp sunflower or olive oil
1 onion, finely chopped
2 tsp garlic purée
1 tsp ground ginger
1 tsp ground fennel seeds
$1/2$ tsp ground turmeric
$1/2$–1 tsp chilli powder
125 g/$4^1/2$ oz raw cashew
  nuts, soaked in 150 ml/
  5 fl oz boiling water for
  20 minutes
150 ml/5 fl oz double cream
1 tbsp crushed pistachio
  nuts, to garnish

method

1 Put the lamb mince in a mixing bowl and add the yogurt, egg, cardamom, nutmeg, pepper, mint and salt. Knead the mince until it is smooth and velvety. Chill for 30–40 minutes, then divide into quarters. Make five balls out of each quarter and roll them between your palms to make them smooth and neat.

2 Bring the 300 ml/10 fl oz water to the boil in a large shallow pan and add all the whole spices and the bay leaves. Arrange the meatballs in a single layer in the spiced liquid, reduce the heat to medium, cover the pan and cook for 12–15 minutes. Remove the meatballs, cover and keep hot. Strain the spiced stock and set aside.

3 Wipe out the pan and add the oil. Place over a medium heat and add the onion and garlic purée. Cook until the mixture begins to brown and add the ground ginger, ground fennel seeds, turmeric and chilli powder. Stir-fry for 2–3 minutes, then add the strained stock and meatballs. Bring to the boil, reduce the heat to low, cover and simmer for 10–12 minutes.

4 Meanwhile, purée the cashews in a blender and add to the meatball mixture along with the cream. Simmer for a further 5–6 minutes, then remove from the heat. Garnish with crushed pistachio nuts and serve.

lamb kebabs

ingredients

SERVES 8

55 g/2 oz raw cashew nuts

3 tbsp double cream

1 egg

1 tbsp gram flour

2 fresh green chillies, roughly
　　chopped

2 shallots, roughly chopped

450 g/1 lb fresh lamb mince

1 tsp salt, or to taste

2 tsp garlic purée

2 tsp ginger purée

1 tsp ground cumin

1 tsp garam masala

1 tbsp chopped fresh mint
　　leaves

2 tbsp chopped fresh
　　coriander leaves

$1/2$ red pepper, deseeded and
　　finely chopped

2 tbsp vegetable oil,
　　for brushing

55 g/2 oz butter, melted

salad and chutney, to serve

method

1 Put the cashew nuts in a heatproof bowl, cover with boiling water and leave to soak for 20 minutes. Drain and put in a food processor. Add the cream and egg and process the ingredients to a coarse mixture.

2 Add all the remaining ingredients, except the herbs, red pepper, oil and butter, and process until thoroughly mixed. Transfer the mixture to a large bowl. Add the herbs and red pepper and mix well. Cover and chill in the refrigerator for 30–40 minutes.

3 Preheat the grill to high. Brush a grill rack and 8 metal skewers lightly with oil. Have a bowl of cold water ready.

4 Divide the chilled mixture into 8 equal-sized portions. Dip your hands into the bowl of cold water – this will stop the mixture sticking to your fingers when you are moulding it onto the skewers. Carefully mould each portion onto a skewer, forming it into a 15-cm/6-inch sausage shape. Arrange the kebabs on the prepared rack and cook under the preheated grill for 4 minutes. Brush with half the melted butter and cook for a further minute. Turn over and cook for 3 minutes. Baste with the remaining melted butter and cook for a further 2 minutes.

5 Remove from the heat and leave the kebabs to rest for 5 minutes before sliding them off the skewers with a knife. Serve with salad and chutney.

kashmiri lamb chops

ingredients

SERVES 4

4 lamb chump chops or
    8 cutlets
300 ml/10 fl oz full-fat milk
1 tbsp ginger purée
$1/2$ tsp pepper
pinch of saffron threads,
    pounded
$1^1/2$ tsp ground fennel seeds
1 tsp ground cumin
$1/2$ tsp chilli powder
4 cloves
2.5-cm/1-inch piece
    cinnamon stick
4 green cardamom pods,
    bruised
1 tsp salt, or to taste
$1/2$ tsp garam masala
1 tbsp fresh mint leaves,
    chopped, or $1/2$ tsp dried
    mint
1 tbsp chopped fresh
    coriander leaves
mixed leaf salad, to serve

method

1 Remove the rind from the chops. Bring enough water to cover the chops to the boil in a medium saucepan. Add the chops, return to the boil and cook for 2–3 minutes. Drain the chops, rinse and drain again.

2 Put the drained chops into a large non-stick saucepan and add all the remaining ingredients, except the garam masala and herbs. Place the saucepan over a medium heat and stir until the milk begins to bubble. Reduce the heat to low, cover and cook for 30 minutes, turning the chops occasionally.

3 Remove from the heat. Using tongs, lift the chops out of the saucepan and shake the cooking liquid back into the saucepan. Strain the liquid and return to the saucepan with the chops. Cook over a medium heat, turning frequently, for 7–8 minutes, until the liquid has evaporated and the chops are browned.

4 Sprinkle the garam masala evenly over the chops and add the mint and coriander. Stir and cook for 1 minute. Serve immediately with a mixed salad.

sesame lamb chops

ingredients

SERVES 4

12 lamb chops, such as best
    end of neck or middle neck
vegetable oil, for brushing
1^1/$_2$ tbsp sesame seeds
pepper
lime wedges, to serve

marinade

4 tbsp natural yogurt
2 tbsp grated lemon rind
1^1/$_2$ tsp ground cumin
1^1/$_2$ tsp ground coriander
^{1}/$_4$ tsp chilli powder
salt

method

1 To make the marinade, put the yogurt, lemon rind, cumin, coriander, chilli powder and salt to taste in a large bowl and stir together.

2 Use a sharp knife to trim any fat from the edge of the lamb chops and scrape the meat off the long piece of bone. Using a rolling pin or the end of a large chef's knife, pound each chop until it is about 5 mm/^{1}/4 inch thick.

3 Add the chops to the bowl and use your hands to stir around until they are coated in the marinade. Leave to marinate for 20 minutes at room temperature, or cover the bowl and refrigerate for up to 4 hours. Return to room temperature before cooking.

4 Preheat the grill to its highest setting and brush the grill rack lightly with oil.

5 Arrange the chops on the grill rack in a single layer, then sprinkle the sesame seeds over each. Grill the chops about 10 cm/ 4 inches from the heat for about 7 minutes, without turning, for medium.

6 Grind pepper over the chops and serve with lime wedges for squeezing over.

marinated lamb brochettes

ingredients

SERVES 4

700 g/1 lb 9 oz boned leg of lamb, cut into 2.5-cm/1-inch cubes

2 tbsp light malt vinegar

$1/2$ tsp salt, or to taste

1 tbsp garlic purée

1 tbsp ginger purée

115 g/4 oz whole milk natural yogurt, strained, or Greek-style yogurt

1 tbsp gram flour

1 tsp ground cumin

1 tsp garam masala

$1/2$–1 tsp chilli powder

$1/2$ tsp ground turmeric

3 tbsp olive or sunflower oil, plus 1 tbsp for brushing

$1/2$ red pepper, deseeded and cut into 2.5-cm/1-inch pieces

$1/2$ green pepper, deseeded and cut into 2.5-cm/1-inch pieces

8 shallots, halved

55 g/2 oz butter, melted

lemon wedges, to serve

method

1 Put the meat in a large non-metallic bowl and add the vinegar, salt and garlic and ginger purées. Mix together thoroughly, cover and leave to marinate in the refrigerator for 30 minutes.

2 Put the yogurt and gram flour in a separate bowl and beat together with a fork until smooth. Add the cumin, garam masala, chilli powder, turmeric and oil and mix together thoroughly. Add the yogurt mixture to the marinated meat, then add the peppers and shallots and stir until well blended. Cover and leave to marinate in the refrigerator for 2–3 hours, or overnight. Return to room temperature before cooking.

3 Preheat the grill to high. Line the grill pan with a piece of foil. Brush the rack and 4 metal skewers with the oil.

4 Thread the marinated lamb, peppers and shallots alternately onto the prepared skewers. Place the skewers on the prepared rack and cook under the preheated grill for 4 minutes. Brush generously with half the melted butter and cook for a further 2 minutes. Turn over and cook for 3–4 minutes. Brush with the remaining butter and cook for a further 2 minutes.

5 Balance the brochettes over a large saucepan or frying pan and leave to rest for 5–6 minutes before sliding off the skewers with a knife. Serve with the lemon wedges.

coriander lamb kebabs

ingredients

SERVES 4–6

700 g/1 lb 9 oz fresh lamb
  mince
1 onion, grated
3 tbsp finely chopped fresh
  coriander leaves and stems
3 tbsp finely chopped fresh
  mint
3 tbsp gram flour
1^1/$_2$ tbsp ground almonds
2.5-cm/1-inch piece fresh
  ginger, grated
3 tbsp lemon juice
2 tbsp natural yogurt
2 tsp ground cumin
2 tsp ground coriander
1^1/$_2$ tsp salt
1^1/$_2$ tsp garam masala
1 tsp ground cinnamon
pepper, to taste
vegetable oil, for brushing
lemon wedges, to serve

method

1 Place all the ingredients except the oil in a large bowl and use your hands to incorporate everything until the texture is smooth. Cover the bowl with a tea towel and leave to stand for about 45 minutes at room temperature.

2 With wet hands, divide the lamb mixture into 24 equal-sized balls. Working with one ball at a time, mould it around a long, flat metal skewer. Continue until all the mixture has been used and you have filled 4 or 6 skewers.

3 Preheat the grill to high. Lightly brush the grill rack with oil. Add the skewers and grill for 5–7 minutes, turning frequently, until the lamb is completely cooked through and not at all pink when you pierce it with the point of a knife. Serve with lemon wedges for squeezing over.

kheema matar

ingredients

SERVES 4–6

30 g/1 oz ghee or 2 tbsp
    vegetable or groundnut oil
2 tsp cumin seeds
1 large onion, finely chopped
1 tbsp garlic and ginger paste
2 bay leaves
1 tsp mild, medium or hot
    curry powder, to taste
2 tomatoes, deseeded and
    chopped
1 tsp ground coriander
$1/4$–$1/2$ tsp chilli powder
$1/4$ tsp ground turmeric
pinch of sugar
$1/2$ teaspoon salt
$1/2$ teaspoon pepper
500 g/1 lb 2 oz fresh lean
    lamb or beef mince
250 g/9 oz frozen peas,
    straight from the freezer

method

1 Melt the ghee in a flameproof casserole or large frying pan with a tight-fitting lid. Add the cumin seeds and cook, stirring, for 30 seconds, or until they start to crackle.

2 Stir in the onion, garlic and ginger paste, bay leaves and curry powder and continue to stir-fry until the fat separates.

3 Stir in the tomatoes and cook for 1–2 minutes. Stir in the coriander, chilli powder, turmeric, sugar, salt and pepper and stir around for 30 seconds.

4 Add the lamb and cook for 5 minutes, using a wooden spoon to break up the meat, or until it is no longer pink. Reduce the heat and simmer, stirring occasionally, for 10 minutes.

5 Add the peas and continue simmering for a further 10–15 minutes, until the peas are thawed and hot. If there is too much liquid left in the pan, increase the heat and let it bubble for a few minutes until it reduces.

balti beef

ingredients

SERVES 4–6

30 g/1 oz ghee or 2 tbsp
    vegetable or groundnut oil
1 large onion, chopped
2 garlic cloves, crushed
2 large red peppers,
    deseeded and chopped
600 g/1 lb 5 oz boneless
    beef, such as sirloin,
    thinly sliced
fresh coriander sprigs,
    to garnish
Indian bread, to serve

balti sauce

30 g/1 oz ghee or 2 tbsp
    vegetable or groundnut oil
2 large onions, chopped
1 tbsp garlic and ginger paste
400 g/14 oz canned chopped
    tomatoes
1 tsp ground paprika
$1/2$ tsp ground turmeric
$1/2$ tsp ground cumin
$1/2$ tsp ground coriander
$1/4$ tsp chilli powder
$1/4$ tsp ground cardamom
1 bay leaf
salt and pepper

method

1 To make the balti sauce, melt the ghee in a wok or large frying pan over a medium–high heat. Add the onions and garlic and ginger paste and stir-fry for about 5 minutes, until the onions are golden brown. Stir in the tomatoes, then add the paprika, turmeric, cumin, coriander, chilli powder, cardamom, bay leaf and salt and pepper to taste. Bring to the boil, stirring, then reduce the heat and simmer for 20 minutes, stirring occasionally.

2 Leave the sauce to cool slightly, then remove the bay leaf and pour the mixture into a food processor or blender and whizz to a smooth sauce.

3 Wipe out the wok and return it to a medium–high heat. Add the ghee and melt. Add the onion and garlic and stir-fry for 5–8 minutes, until golden brown. Add the red peppers and continue stir-frying for 2 minutes.

4 Stir in the beef and continue stirring for 2 minutes, until it starts to turn brown. Add the balti sauce and bring to the boil. Reduce the heat and simmer for 5 minutes, or until the sauce slightly reduces again and the peppers are tender. Adjust the seasoning, if necessary. Garnish with coriander sprigs and serve with Indian bread.

beef madras

ingredients

SERVES 4–6

1–2 dried red chillies

2 tsp ground coriander

2 tsp ground turmeric

1 tsp black mustard seeds

$^1/_2$ tsp ground ginger

$^1/_4$ tsp pepper

140 g/5 oz creamed coconut, grated, dissolved in 300 ml/ 10 fl oz boiling water

55 g/2 oz ghee or 4 tbsp vegetable or groundnut oil

2 onions, chopped

3 large garlic cloves, chopped

700 g/1 lb 9 oz lean stewing steak, such as chuck, trimmed and cut into 5-cm/2-inch cubes

250 ml/9 fl oz beef stock

lemon juice

salt

poppadoms, to serve

method

1 Depending on how hot you want this dish to be, chop the chillies with or without any seeds. The more seeds you include, the hotter the dish will be. Put the chopped chilli and any seeds in a small bowl with the coriander, turmeric, mustard seeds, ginger and pepper and stir in a little of the dissolved creamed coconut to make a thin paste.

2 Melt the ghee in a flameproof casserole or large frying pan with a tight-fitting lid over a medium–high heat. Add the onions and garlic and cook for 5–8 minutes, stirring frequently, until the onions are golden brown. Add the spice paste and stir around for 2 minutes, or until you can smell the aromas.

3 Add the meat and stock and bring to the boil. Reduce the heat to its lowest level, cover tightly and simmer for 1^1/2 hours, or until the beef is tender. Check occasionally that the meat isn't catching on the base of the pan and stir in a little extra water or stock, if necessary.

4 Uncover the pan and stir in the remaining dissolved coconut cream with the lemon juice and salt to taste. Bring to the boil, stirring, then reduce the heat again and simmer, still uncovered, until the sauce reduces slightly. Serve with poppadoms.

beef korma with almonds

ingredients

SERVES 6

300 ml/10 fl oz vegetable oil

3 onions, finely chopped

1 kg/2 lb 4 oz lean beef, cubed

1$\frac{1}{2}$ tsp garam masala

1$\frac{1}{2}$ tsp ground coriander

1$\frac{1}{2}$ tsp finely chopped fresh
   ginger

1$\frac{1}{2}$ tsp crushed garlic

1 tsp salt

150 ml/5 fl oz natural yogurt

2 whole cloves

3 green cardamom pods

4 black peppercorns

600 ml/1 pint water

chapatis, to serve

to garnish

chopped blanched almonds

sliced fresh green chillies

chopped fresh coriander

method

1 Heat the oil in a large heavy-based frying pan. Add the onions and stir-fry for 8–10 minutes, until golden. Remove half of the onions and reserve.

2 Add the meat to the remaining onions in the frying pan and stir-fry for 5 minutes. Remove the frying pan from the heat.

3 Mix the garam masala, ground coriander, ginger, garlic, salt and yogurt together in a large bowl. Gradually add the meat to the yogurt and spice mixture and mix to coat the meat on all sides. Place the meat mixture in the frying pan, return to the heat, and stir-fry for 5–7 minutes, or until the mixture is nearly brown.

4 Add the cloves, cardamom pods and peppercorns. Add the water, reduce the heat, cover and simmer for 45–60 minutes. If the water has completely evaporated but the meat is still not tender enough, add another 300 ml/10 fl oz water and cook for a further 10–15 minutes, stirring occasionally.

5 Transfer to serving dishes and garnish with the reserved onions, chopped almonds, chillies and fresh coriander. Serve with chapatis.

beef dhansak

ingredients

SERVES 6

2 tbsp ghee or vegetable oil

2 onions, chopped

3 garlic cloves, finely chopped

2 tsp ground coriander

2 tsp ground cumin

2 tsp garam masala

1 tsp ground turmeric

450 g/1 lb courgettes, peeled
    and chopped, or bitter
    gourd or pumpkin, peeled,
    deseeded and chopped

1 aubergine, peeled and
    chopped

4 curry leaves

225 g/8 oz red split lentils
    (masoor dhal)

1 litre/1³/4 pints water

1 kg/2 lb 4 oz stewing steak,
    diced

salt

fresh coriander leaves,
    to garnish

method

1 Heat the ghee in a large heavy-based saucepan. Add the onions and garlic and cook over a low heat, stirring occasionally, for 8–10 minutes, or until golden. Stir in the ground coriander, cumin, garam masala and turmeric and cook, stirring constantly, for 2 minutes.

2 Add the courgettes, aubergine, curry leaves, lentils and water. Bring to the boil, then reduce the heat, cover and simmer for 30 minutes, or until the vegetables are tender. Remove the saucepan from the heat and leave to cool slightly. Transfer the mixture to a food processor, in batches if necessary, and process until smooth. Return the mixture to the saucepan and season to taste with salt.

3 Add the steak to the saucepan and bring to the boil. Reduce the heat, cover and simmer for 1¹/4 hours. Remove the lid and continue to simmer for a further 30 minutes, or until the sauce is thick and the steak is tender. Serve garnished with coriander leaves.

pork vindaloo

ingredients

SERVES 4

2–6 dried red chillies, torn

5 cloves

2.5-cm/1-inch piece cinnamon
  stick, broken up

4 green cardamom pods

$^1/_2$ tsp black peppercorns

$^1/_2$ mace blade

$^1/_4$ nutmeg, lightly crushed

1 tsp cumin seeds

1$^1/_2$ tsp coriander seeds

$^1/_2$ tsp fenugreek seeds

2 tsp garlic purée

1 tbsp ginger purée

3 tbsp cider vinegar or white
  wine vinegar

1 tbsp tamarind juice or juice
  of $^1/_2$ lime

700 g/1 lb 9 oz boneless leg
  of pork, cut into 2.5-cm/
  1-inch cubes

4 tbsp sunflower or olive oil,
  plus 2 tsp

2 large onions, finely chopped

250 ml/9 fl oz warm water,
  plus 4 tbsp

1 tsp salt, or to taste

1 tsp soft dark brown sugar

2 large garlic cloves, finely
  sliced

8–10 fresh or dried curry
  leaves

method

1 Grind the first 10 ingredients (all the spices) to a fine powder in a spice grinder. Transfer the ground spices to a bowl and add the garlic and ginger purées, vinegar and tamarind juice. Mix together to form a paste.

2 Put the pork in a large non-metallic bowl and rub about one quarter of the spice paste into the meat. Cover and leave to marinate in the refrigerator for 30–40 minutes.

3 Heat the 4 tablespoons of oil in a medium heavy-based saucepan over a medium heat, add the onions and cook, stirring frequently, for 8–10 minutes, until lightly browned. Add the remaining spice paste and cook, stirring constantly, for 5–6 minutes. Add 2 tablespoons of the warm water and cook until it evaporates. Repeat with another 2 tablespoons of water.

4 Add the marinated pork and cook over medium–high heat for 5–6 minutes, until the meat changes colour. Add the salt, sugar and the 250 ml/9 fl oz warm water. Bring to the boil, then reduce the heat to low, cover and simmer for 50–55 minutes.

5 Meanwhile, heat the 2 teaspoons of oil in a small saucepan over a low heat. Add the sliced garlic and cook, stirring, until it begins to brown. Add the curry leaves and leave to sizzle for 15–20 seconds. Stir the garlic mixture into the vindaloo. Serve immediately.

railway pork & vegetables

ingredients

SERVES 4–6

40 g/1$\frac{1}{2}$ oz ghee or 3 tbsp
    vegetable or groundnut oil
1 large onion, finely chopped
4 green cardamom pods
3 cloves
1 cinnamon stick
1 tbsp garlic and ginger paste
2 tsp garam masala
$\frac{1}{4}$–$\frac{1}{2}$ tsp chilli powder
$\frac{1}{2}$ tsp ground asafoetida
2 tsp salt, or to taste
600 g/1 lb 5 oz fresh lean
    pork mince
1 potato, scrubbed and cut
    into 5-mm/$\frac{1}{4}$-inch dice
400 g/14 oz canned chopped
    tomatoes
125 ml/4 fl oz water
1 bay leaf
1 large carrot, coarsely grated
salt and pepper

method

1 Melt the ghee in a flameproof casserole or large frying pan with a tight-fitting lid over a medium heat. Add the onion and cook, stirring occasionally, for 5–8 minutes, until golden brown. Add the cardamom pods, cloves and cinnamon stick and cook, stirring, for 1 minute, or until you can smell the aromas.

2 Add the garlic and ginger paste, garam masala, chilli powder, asafoetida and salt and stir around for a further minute. Add the pork and cook for 5 minutes, or until no longer pink, using a wooden spoon to break up the meat.

3 Add the potato, tomatoes, water and bay leaf and bring to the boil, stirring. Reduce the heat to the lowest level, cover tightly and simmer for 15 minutes. Stir in the carrot and simmer for a further 5 minutes, or until the potato and carrot are tender. Taste and adjust the seasoning, adding salt and pepper if necessary, and serve.

pork with cinnamon & fenugreek

ingredients

SERVES 4

1 tsp ground coriander
1 tsp ground cumin
1 tsp chilli powder
1 tbsp dried fenugreek leaves
1 tsp ground fenugreek
150 ml/5 fl oz natural yogurt
450 g/1 lb diced pork fillet
4 tbsp ghee or vegetable oil
1 large onion, sliced
5-cm/2-inch piece fresh
   ginger, finely chopped
4 garlic cloves, finely chopped
1 cinnamon stick
6 green cardamom pods
6 whole cloves
2 bay leaves
175 ml/6 fl oz water
salt

method

1 Mix the coriander, cumin, chilli powder, dried fenugreek, ground fenugreek and yogurt together in a small bowl. Place the pork in a large, shallow non-metallic dish and add the spice mixture, turning well to coat. Cover with clingfilm and leave to marinate in the refrigerator for 30 minutes.

2 Melt the ghee in a large heavy-based saucepan. Cook the onion over a low heat, stirring occasionally, for 5 minutes, or until soft. Add the ginger, garlic, cinnamon stick, cardamom pods, cloves and bay leaves and cook, stirring constantly, for 2 minutes, or until the spices give off their aroma. Add the meat with its marinade and the water, and season to taste with salt. Bring to the boil, reduce the heat, cover and simmer for 30 minutes.

3 Transfer the meat mixture to a preheated wok or large heavy-based frying pan and cook over a low heat, stirring constantly, until dry and tender. If necessary, occasionally sprinkle with a little water to prevent it from sticking to the wok. Serve immediately.

pork with tamarind

ingredients

SERVES 6

55 g/2 oz dried tamarind,
   roughly chopped
500 ml/18 fl oz boiling water
2 fresh green chillies, deseeded
   and roughly chopped
2 onions, roughly chopped
2 garlic cloves, roughly
   chopped
1 lemon grass stalk, bulb end
   roughly chopped
2 tbsp ghee or vegetable oil
1 tbsp ground coriander
1 tsp ground turmeric
1 tsp ground cardamom
1 tsp chilli powder
1 tsp ginger purée
1 cinnamon stick
1 kg/2 lb 4 oz diced pork fillet
1 tbsp chopped fresh coriander,
   plus extra sprigs to garnish
sliced fresh red chillies,
   to garnish

method

1 Place the dried tamarind in a small bowl, pour in the boiling water and mix well. Leave to soak for 30 minutes.

2 Strain the soaking liquid through a sieve into a clean bowl, pressing down the pulp with the back of a wooden spoon. Discard the pulp. Pour 1 tablespoon of the tamarind liquid into a food processor and add the green chillies, onions, garlic and lemon grass and process until smooth.

3 Heat the ghee in a large heavy-based saucepan. Add the chilli and onion paste, ground coriander, turmeric, ground cardamom, chilli powder, ginger purée and cinnamon stick and cook, stirring, for 2 minutes, or until the spices give off their aroma.

4 Add the pork and cook, stirring constantly, until lightly browned and well coated in the spice mixture. Pour in the remaining tamarind liquid, bring to the boil, then reduce the heat, cover and simmer for 30 minutes. Remove the lid from the saucepan and simmer for a further 30 minutes, or until the pork is tender. Stir in the chopped coriander and serve garnished with coriander sprigs and sliced red chillies.

fish & seafood

The seas around India supply a wealth of fish and seafood and, hardly surprisingly, fish is on the menu every day in the south and west of the country. Indian cooks are used to preparing whatever looks tastiest and freshest in the day's catch, although pomfret and prawns are particular favourites. This flexibility of approach makes it easy to adapt traditional recipes for varieties of fish more widely available in the West.

It is, perhaps, surprising how well fish and seafood go with all kinds of spices, whether in a fragrant mix with coconut milk, yogurt or lime juice or in a sizzling hot chilli sauce. Bengal is famous for its fish recipes and its use of pungent mustard oil – so be warned if you try a Bengali fish dish.

Fish is prepared in many different ways so there is always something interesting on the menu. It may be pan-fried, deep-fried or grilled whole, as fillets or in strips, (often after coating with turmeric or other spices), stewed with mixed vegetables or beans, stir-fried, made into a flavoursome curry, cooked on skewers or pickled and served cold. Seafood dishes are just as varied and delicious, whether a spicy curry of tiger prawns or mussels cooked Goan-style in a delicate coconut sauce.

balti fish curry

ingredients

SERVES 4–6

900 g/2 lb thick fish fillets,
    such as monkfish, grey
    mullet, cod or haddock,
    rinsed and cut into large
    chunks
2 bay leaves, torn
140 g/5 oz ghee or 150 ml/
    5 fl oz vegetable or
    groundnut oil
2 large onions, chopped
1/2 tbsp salt
150 ml/5 fl oz water
chopped fresh coriander,
    to garnish
Indian bread, to serve

marinade

1/2 tbsp garlic and ginger
    paste
1 fresh green chilli, deseeded
    and chopped
1 tsp ground coriander
1 tsp ground cumin
1/2 tsp ground turmeric
1/4–1/2 tsp chilli powder
1 tbsp water
salt

method

1 To make the marinade, mix the garlic and ginger paste, green chilli, ground coriander, cumin, turmeric and chilli powder together with salt to taste in a large bowl. Gradually stir in the water to form a thin paste. Add the fish chunks and smear with the marinade. Tuck the bay leaves underneath and leave to marinate in the refrigerator for at least 30 minutes, or up to 4 hours.

2 Remove the fish from the refrigerator 15 minutes in advance of cooking. Melt the ghee in a wok or large frying pan over a medium–high heat. Add the onions, sprinkle with the salt and cook, stirring frequently, for 8 minutes, or until they are very soft and golden.

3 Gently add the fish with its marinade and the bay leaves to the pan and stir in the water. Bring to the boil, then immediately reduce the heat and cook the fish for 4–5 minutes, spooning the sauce over the fish and carefully moving the chunks around until they are cooked through and the flesh flakes easily. Garnish with coriander and serve with Indian bread.

bengali-style fish

ingredients

SERVES 4–8

1 tsp ground turmeric

1 tsp salt

1 kg/2 lb 4 oz cod fillet, skinned
    and cut into pieces

6 tbsp mustard oil

4 fresh green chillies

1 tsp finely chopped fresh
    ginger

1 tsp crushed garlic

2 onions, finely chopped

2 tomatoes, finely chopped

450 ml/16 fl oz water

chopped fresh coriander,
    to garnish

Indian bread, to serve

method

1 Mix the turmeric and salt together in a small bowl, then spoon the mixture over the fish pieces.

2 Heat the mustard oil in a large heavy-based frying pan. Add the fish and fry until pale yellow. Remove the fish with a slotted spoon and reserve.

3 Place the chillies, ginger, garlic, onions and tomatoes in a mortar and grind with a pestle to make a paste. Alternatively, place the ingredients in a food processor and process until smooth.

4 Transfer the spice paste to a clean frying pan and dry-fry until golden brown.

5 Remove the frying pan from the heat and place the fish pieces in the paste without breaking up the fish. Return the frying pan to the heat, add the water and cook over a medium heat for 15–20 minutes. Transfer to a warmed serving dish, garnish with chopped coriander and serve with Indian bread.

goan-style seafood curry

ingredients

SERVES 4–6

3 tbsp vegetable or groundnut
  oil
1 tbsp black mustard seeds
12 fresh or 1 tbsp dried curry
  leaves
6 shallots, finely chopped
1 garlic clove, crushed
1 tsp ground turmeric
$1/2$ tsp ground coriander
$1/4$–$1/2$ tsp chilli powder
140 g/5 oz creamed coconut,
  grated and dissolved in
  300 ml/10 fl oz boiling
  water
500 g/1 lb 2 oz skinless,
  boneless white fish, such
  as monkfish or cod, cut
  into large chunks
450 g/1 lb large raw prawns,
  peeled and deveined
finely grated rind and juice
  of 1 lime
salt

method

1 Heat the oil in a wok or large frying pan over a high heat. Add the mustard seeds and stir them around for about 1 minute, or until they pop. Stir in the curry leaves.

2 Add the shallots and garlic and stir for about 5 minutes, or until the shallots are golden. Stir in the turmeric, coriander and chilli powder and continue stirring for about 30 seconds.

3 Add the dissolved creamed coconut. Bring to the boil, then reduce the heat to medium and stir for about 2 minutes.

4 Reduce the heat to low, add the fish and simmer for 1 minute, spooning the sauce over the fish and very gently stirring it around. Add the prawns and continue to simmer for a further 4–5 minutes, until the fish flakes easily and the prawns turn pink and curl.

5 Add half the lime juice, then taste and add more lime juice and salt to taste. Sprinkle with the lime rind and serve.

steamed fish with coriander chutney

ingredients

SERVES 4

1 quantity coriander chutney
   (see page 198)
1 large fresh banana leaf
vegetable or groundnut oil
4 white fish fillets, such as
   pomfret or sole, about
   140 g/5 oz each
salt and pepper
lime or lemon wedges,
   to serve

method

1 Prepare the coriander chutney at least 2 hours in advance to allow the flavours to blend.

2 Meanwhile, cut the banana leaf into 4 squares large enough to fold comfortably around the fish to make tight parcels.

3 Working with one piece of leaf at a time, very lightly rub the bottom with oil. Put one of the fish fillets in the centre of the oiled side, flesh-side up. Spread one quarter of the coriander chutney over the top and season to taste with salt and pepper.

4 Fold one side of the leaf over the fish, then fold the opposite side over. Turn the leaf so the folded edges are top and bottom. Fold the right-hand end of the leaf parcel into the centre, then fold over the left-hand side. Trim the ends if the parcel becomes too bulky.

5 Use 2 wooden skewers to close the leaf parcel. Repeat with the remaining ingredients and banana leaf squares.

6 Place a steamer large enough to hold the parcels in a single layer over a pan of boiling water, without letting the water touch the fish. Add the fish, cover the pan and steam for 15 minutes. Make sure the fish is cooked through and flakes easily.

7 Serve the fish parcels with lime or lemon wedges.

fish pakoras

ingredients

SERVES 4

1/2 tsp salt

2 tbsp lemon juice or distilled
    white vinegar

700 g/1 lb 9 oz skinless white
    fish fillets, such as cod,
    halibut or monkfish, rinsed,
    patted dry and cut into
    large chunks

vegetable or groundnut oil,
    for deep-frying

pepper

lemon wedges, to serve

batter

140 g/5 oz gram flour

seeds from 4 green
    cardamom pods

large pinch of ground turmeric

large pinch of bicarbonate
    of soda

finely grated rind of 1 lemon

175 ml/6 fl oz water

salt and pepper

method

1 Combine the salt, lemon juice and pepper to taste and rub all over the fish chunks, then set aside in a non-metallic bowl and leave to stand for 20–30 minutes.

2 Meanwhile, to make the batter put the gram flour in a bowl and stir in the seeds from the cardamom pods, the turmeric, bicarbonate of soda, lemon rind and salt and pepper to taste. Make a well in the centre and gradually stir in the water until a thin batter forms, similar in consistency to single cream.

3 Gently stir the pieces of fish into the batter, taking care not to break them up.

4 Heat enough oil for deep-frying in a wok, deep-fat fryer or large heavy-based saucepan to 180°C/350°F, or until a cube of bread browns in 30 seconds. Remove the fish pieces from the batter and let the excess batter drip back into the bowl. Without overcrowding the pan, drop fish pieces in the hot oil and fry for about 2 1/2–3 minutes, until golden brown.

5 Use a slotted spoon to remove the fried fish pieces from the oil and drain on crumpled kitchen paper. Continue until all the fish is fried, then serve hot with the lemon wedges.

pomfret in chilli yogurt

ingredients

SERVES 4

2 tbsp vegetable or groundnut
    oil

1 large onion, sliced

4-cm/1^1/$_2$-inch piece fresh
    ginger, finely chopped

^{1}/$_2$ tsp salt

^{1}/$_4$ tsp ground turmeric

pinch of ground cinnamon

pinch of ground cloves

200 ml/7 fl oz natural yogurt

1 tbsp plain flour

small pinch of chilli powder

4 skinless pomfret fillets,
    about 150 g/5^1/$_2$ oz each,
    wiped dry

30 g/1 oz ghee or 2 tbsp
    vegetable or groundnut oil

salt and pepper

2 fresh fat green chillies,
    deseeded and finely
    chopped, to garnish

method

1 Heat the oil in a large frying pan over a medium–high heat. Add the onion and fry, stirring, for 8 minutes, or until it is soft and dark golden brown. Add the ginger and stir around for a further minute.

2 Stir in the salt, turmeric, cinnamon and cloves and continue stirring for 30 seconds. Remove the pan from the heat and stir in the yogurt, a little at a time, beating constantly.

3 Transfer the yogurt mixture to a blender or food processor and whizz until a paste forms.

4 Season the flour with chilli powder and salt and pepper to taste. Place it on a plate and lightly dust the fish fillets on both sides.

5 Melt the ghee in the wiped pan over a medium–high heat. When it is bubbling, reduce the heat to medium and add the fish fillets in a single layer. Fry for 2^1/$_2$ minutes, or until golden, then turn them over.

6 Continue frying for a further minute, then return the yogurt sauce to the pan and reheat, stirring. When the fillets flake easily and are cooked through and the sauce is hot, transfer to plates and sprinkle with the green chilli.

fish in tomato & chilli sauce with fried onion

ingredients

SERVES 4

700 g/1 lb 9 oz tilapia fillets, cut into 5-cm/2-inch pieces

2 tbsp lemon juice

1 tsp salt, or to taste

1 tsp ground turmeric

4 tbsp sunflower or olive oil, plus extra for shallow-frying

2 tsp granulated sugar

1 large onion, finely chopped

2 tsp ginger purée

2 tsp garlic purée

$1/2$ tsp ground fennel seeds

1 tsp ground coriander

$1/2$–1 tsp chilli powder

175 g/6 oz canned chopped tomatoes

300 ml/10 fl oz warm water

2–3 tbsp chopped fresh coriander leaves

cooked basmati rice, to serve

method

1 Lay the fish on a plate and gently rub in the lemon juice, half the salt and half the turmeric. Set aside for 15–20 minutes.

2 Pour enough oil to cover the base of a frying pan to a depth of about 1 cm/$1/2$ inch and place over a medium–high heat. Fry the pieces of fish, in a single layer, until well browned on both sides. Drain on kitchen paper.

3 Heat the 4 tablespoons of oil in a medium saucepan over a medium heat and add the sugar. Allow it to brown, watching it carefully because once it browns it will blacken quickly. Add the onion and cook for 5 minutes, until soft. Add the ginger and garlic purées, and cook for a further 3–4 minutes.

4 Add the ground fennel, ground coriander, chilli powder and the remaining turmeric. Cook for about a minute, then add half the tomatoes. Cook until the tomato juice has evaporated, then add the remaining tomatoes. Continue to cook, stirring, until the oil separates from the spice paste.

5 Pour in the warm water and add the remaining salt. Bring to the boil, then add the fish, stir gently, and reduce the heat to low. Cook, uncovered, for 5–6 minutes, then stir in the chopped coriander and remove from the heat. Serve with cooked basmati rice.

fish korma

ingredients

SERVES 4

700 g/1 lb 9 oz tilapia fillets,
    cut into 5-cm/2-inch pieces

1 tbsp lemon juice

1 tsp salt

55 g/2 oz raw unsalted cashews

3 tbsp sunflower or olive oil

5-cm/2-inch piece cinnamon
    stick, halved

4 green cardamom pods,
    bruised

2 cloves

1 large onion, finely chopped

1–2 fresh green chillies,
    chopped (deseeded if
    you like)

2 tsp ginger purée

2 tsp garlic purée

150 ml/5 fl oz single cream

55 g/2 oz whole milk natural
    yogurt

$1/4$ tsp ground turmeric

$1/2$ tsp sugar

1 tbsp toasted flaked
    almonds, to garnish

Indian bread, to serve

method

1 Place the fish in a large plate and gently rub in the lemon juice and $1/2$ teaspoon of the salt. Set aside for 20 minutes. Put the cashews in a bowl, cover with boiling water and leave to soak for 15 minutes.

2 Heat the oil in a wide shallow pan over a low heat and add the cinnamon, cardamom and cloves. Let them sizzle for 30–40 seconds.

3 Add the onion, chillies and ginger and garlic purées. Increase the heat slightly and cook, stirring frequently, for 9–10 minutes, until the onion is very soft.

4 Meanwhile, drain the cashews and purée them with the cream and yogurt.

5 Stir the turmeric into the onion mixture and add the puréed ingredients, the remaining salt and the sugar. Mix thoroughly and arrange the fish in the sauce in a single layer. Bring to a slow simmer, cover the pan and cook for 5 minutes. Remove the lid and shake the pan gently from side to side. Spoon some of the sauce over the pieces of fish. Re-cover and cook for a further 3–4 minutes.

6 Transfer to a serving dish and garnish with the toasted almonds. Serve with Indian bread.

goan fish curry

ingredients

SERVES 4

4 skinless salmon fillets,
  about 200 g/7 oz each
1 tsp salt, or to taste
1 tbsp lemon juice
3 tbsp sunflower or olive oil
1 large onion, finely chopped
2 tsp garlic purée
2 tsp ginger purée
$^{1}/_{2}$ tsp ground turmeric
1 tsp ground coriander
$^{1}/_{2}$ tsp ground cumin
$^{1}/_{2}$–1 tsp chilli powder
250 ml/9 fl oz canned
  coconut milk
2–3 fresh green chillies,
  sliced lengthways
  (deseeded if you like)
2 tbsp cider vinegar or white
  wine vinegar
2 tbsp chopped fresh
  coriander leaves
cooked basmati rice,
  to serve

method

1 Cut each salmon fillet in half and lay on a flat surface in a single layer. Sprinkle with half the salt and the lemon juice and rub in gently. Cover and leave to marinate in the refrigerator for 15–20 minutes.

2 Heat the oil in a frying pan over a medium heat, add the onion and cook, stirring frequently to ensure even colouring, for 8–9 minutes, until a pale golden colour.

3 Add the garlic and ginger purées and cook, stirring, for 1 minute, then add the turmeric, ground coriander, cumin and chilli powder and cook, stirring, for 1 minute. Add the coconut milk, chillies and vinegar, then the remaining salt, stir well and simmer, uncovered, for 6–8 minutes.

4 Add the fish and cook gently for 5–6 minutes. Stir in the fresh coriander and remove from the heat. Serve immediately with cooked basmati rice.

fish tikka

ingredients

SERVES 8

pinch of saffron threads,
  pounded
1 tbsp hot milk
85 g/3 oz Greek-style yogurt
1 tbsp garlic purée
1 tbsp ginger purée
1 tsp salt, or to taste
$1/2$ tsp granulated sugar
juice of $1/2$ lemon
$1/2$–1 tsp chilli powder
$1/2$ tsp garam masala
1 tsp ground fennel seeds
2 tsp gram flour
750 g/1 lb 10 oz salmon
  fillets, skinned and cut
  into 5-cm/2-inch cubes
3 tbsp olive oil, plus extra
  for brushing
sliced tomatoes and
  cucumber, to garnish
lemon wedges, to serve

method

1 Soak the pounded saffron in the hot milk for 10 minutes.

2 Put all the remaining ingredients, except the fish and oil, in a bowl and beat with a fork or a wire whisk until smooth. Stir in the saffron and milk, mix well and add the fish cubes. Using a metal spoon, mix gently, turning the fish around until fully coated with the marinade. Cover and leave to marinate in the refrigerator for 2 hours. Return to room temperature before cooking.

3 Preheat the grill to high. Brush a grill rack generously with oil and 8 metal skewers lightly with oil. Line the grill pan with a piece of foil.

4 Thread the fish cubes onto the prepared skewers, leaving a narrow gap between each piece. Arrange on the prepared rack and cook under the preheated grill for 3 minutes. Brush half the 3 tablespoons of oil over the kebabs and cook for a further minute. Turn over and brush any remaining marinade over the fish. Cook for 3 minutes. Brush the remaining oil over the fish and cook for a further 2 minutes, or until the fish is lightly charred.

5 Remove from the heat and leave to rest for 5 minutes. Garnish with tomatoes and cucumber and serve with lemon wedges for squeezing over.

pickled mackerel

ingredients

SERVES 4

4 tbsp vegetable or groundnut
oil, plus extra for brushing

finely grated rind and juice
of 1 lime

4 large mackerel fillets, about
175 g/6 oz each

1^1/$_2$ tsp cumin seeds

1^1/$_2$ tsp black mustard seeds

1^1/$_2$ tsp nigella seeds

1^1/$_2$ tsp fennel seeds

1^1/$_2$ tsp coriander seeds

4-cm/1^1/$_2$-inch piece fresh
ginger, very finely chopped

1^1/$_2$ garlic cloves, very finely
chopped

3 shallots, very finely
chopped

pinch of chilli powder

salt and pepper

fresh red chillies, deseeded
and very finely sliced,
to garnish

lime wedges, to serve

method

1 Mix together 2 tablespoons of the oil, the lime rind and juice and salt and pepper to taste in a non-metallic bowl that will hold the mackerel fillets in a single layer. Add the mackerel fillets and use your hands to cover them in the marinade, then set aside for at least 10 minutes, or cover and chill for up to 4 hours.

2 Meanwhile, preheat the grill to high, and lightly brush a grill rack with oil.

3 Remove the mackerel from the refrigerator 15 minutes in advance of cooking. Put the mackerel on the grill rack, skin-side down, and grill about 10 cm/4 inches from the source of the heat for 6 minutes, or until the flesh is cooked through when pierced with the tip of a knife and flakes easily.

4 Meanwhile, heat the remaining oil in a wok or large frying pan over a medium–high heat. Add the cumin seeds, mustard seeds, nigella seeds, fennel seeds and coriander seeds and stir around until the mustard seeds start to jump and the coriander and cumin seeds just start to brown. Immediately remove the pan from the heat, then stir in the ginger, garlic, shallots and chilli powder and continue stirring for 1 minute.

5 Transfer the mackerel fillets to plates and spoon over the spice mixture. Garnish with red chilli slices and serve with lime wedges for squeezing over.

goan prawn curry with hard-boiled eggs

ingredients

SERVES 4

4 tbsp sunflower or olive oil

1 large onion, finely chopped

2 tsp ginger purée

2 tsp garlic purée

2 tsp ground coriander

$1/2$ tsp ground fennel

$1/2$ tsp ground turmeric

$1/2$–1 tsp chilli powder

$1/2$ tsp pepper

2–3 tbsp water

125 g/4$1/2$ oz canned
   chopped tomatoes

200 ml/7 fl oz coconut milk

1 tsp salt, or to taste

4 hard-boiled eggs

700 g/1 lb 9 oz cooked
   peeled tiger prawns

juice of 1 lime

2–3 tbsp chopped fresh
   coriander leaves

cooked basmati rice, to serve

method

1 Heat the oil in a medium saucepan over a medium–high heat and add the onion. Cook until the onion is soft but not brown. Add the ginger and garlic purées and cook for 2–3 minutes.

2 In a small bowl, mix the ground coriander, ground fennel, turmeric, chilli powder and pepper. Add the water and make a paste. Reduce the heat to medium, add this paste to the onion mixture and cook for 1–2 minutes. Reduce the heat to low and continue to cook for 3–4 minutes.

3 Add half the tomatoes and cook for 2–3 minutes. Add the remaining tomatoes and cook for a further 2–3 minutes.

4 Add the coconut milk and salt, bring to a slow simmer and cook, uncovered, for 6–8 minutes, stirring regularly.

5 Meanwhile, shell the eggs and, using a sharp knife, make 4 slits lengthways on each egg without cutting them through. Add the eggs to the pan along with the prawns. Increase the heat slightly and cook for 6–8 minutes.

6 Stir in the lime juice and half the coriander. Remove from the heat and transfer the curry to a serving dish. Garnish with the remaining coriander and serve with cooked basmati rice.

prawns in coconut milk

ingredients

SERVES 4

4 onions

4 tbsp ghee or vegetable oil

1 tsp garam masala

1 tsp ground turmeric

1 cinnamon stick

2 green cardamom pods, bruised

1/2 tsp chilli powder

2 whole cloves

2 bay leaves

400 ml/14 fl oz coconut milk

1 tsp sugar

500 g/1 lb 2 oz raw tiger prawns, peeled and deveined

salt

pilau rice, to serve

method

1 Finely chop 2 of the onions and grate the other 2. Heat the ghee in a large heavy-based frying pan. Add the garam masala and cook over a low heat, stirring constantly, for 1 minute, or until its aroma is released. Add the chopped onions and cook, stirring occasionally, for 10 minutes, or until golden.

2 Stir in the grated onions, turmeric, cinnamon, cardamom pods, chilli powder, cloves and bay leaves and cook, stirring constantly, for 5 minutes. Stir in half the coconut milk and the sugar and season to taste with salt. Add the prawns and cook, stirring frequently for 8 minutes, or until they have changed colour.

3 Stir in the remaining coconut milk and bring to the boil. Taste and adjust the seasoning, if necessary, and serve immediately with pilau rice.

prawn biryani

ingredients

SERVES 8

1 tsp saffron threads
55 ml/2 fl oz tepid water
2 shallots, roughly chopped
3 garlic cloves, crushed
1 tsp chopped fresh ginger
2 tsp coriander seeds
$^1/_2$ tsp black peppercorns
2 cloves
seeds from 2 green
    cardamom pods
$^1/_2$ cinnamon stick
1 tsp ground turmeric
1 fresh green chilli, chopped
$^1/_2$ tsp salt
2 tbsp ghee
1 tsp black mustard seeds
500 g/1 lb 2 oz raw tiger
    prawns, peeled and
    deveined
300 ml/10 fl oz coconut milk
300 ml/10 fl oz natural yogurt
cooked basmati rice, to serve

to garnish

toasted flaked almonds
sliced spring onion
fresh coriander sprigs

-method

1 Soak the saffron in the tepid water for 10 minutes. Put the shallots, garlic, ginger, coriander seeds, peppercorns, cloves, cardamom seeds, cinnamon stick, turmeric, chilli and salt into a spice grinder or mortar and grind to a paste.

2 Heat the ghee in a saucepan and add the mustard seeds. When they start to pop, add the prawns and stir over a high heat for 1 minute. Stir in the spice mix, then the coconut milk and yogurt. Simmer for 20 minutes.

3 Spoon the prawn mixture into serving bowls. Top with the cooked basmati rice and drizzle over the saffron water. Serve garnished with the flaked almonds, spring onion and coriander sprigs.

tandoori prawns

ingredients

SERVES 4

4 tbsp natural yogurt

2 fresh green chillies,
    deseeded and chopped

$1/2$ tbsp garlic and ginger
    paste

seeds from 4 green
    cardamom pods

2 tsp ground cumin

1 tsp tomato purée

$1/4$ tsp ground turmeric

$1/4$ tsp salt

pinch of chilli powder, ideally
    Kashmiri chilli powder

24 raw tiger prawns, thawed if
    frozen, peeled, deveined
    and tails left intact

oil, for greasing

lemon or lime wedges,
    to serve

method

1 Put the yogurt, chillies and garlic and ginger paste in a small food processor or spice grinder and whizz until a paste forms. Transfer the paste to a large non-metallic bowl and stir in the cardamom seeds, cumin, tomato purée, turmeric, salt and chilli powder.

2 Add the prawns to the bowl and use your hands to make sure they are coated with the yogurt marinade. Cover the bowl with clingfilm and chill for at least 30 minutes, or up to 4 hours.

3 When you are ready to cook, heat a large griddle or frying pan over a high heat until a few drops of water 'dance' when they hit the surface. Use crumpled kitchen paper or a pastry brush to grease the hot pan very lightly with oil.

4 Use tongs to lift the prawns out of the marinade, letting the excess drip back into the bowl, then place the prawns on the griddle and cook for 2 minutes. Flip the prawns over and cook for a further 1–2 minutes, until they turn pink, curl and are opaque all the way through when you cut one. Serve immediately with lemon or lime wedges for squeezing over.

prawn & pineapple tikka

ingredients

SERVES 4

1 tsp cumin seeds

1 tsp coriander seeds

$^1/_2$ tsp fennel seeds

$^1/_2$ tsp yellow mustard seeds

$^1/_4$ tsp fenugreek seeds

$^1/_4$ tsp nigella seeds

pinch of chilli powder

2 tbsp lemon or pineapple juice

12 raw tiger prawns, peeled, deveined and tails left intact

12 bite-sized wedges of fresh or well-drained canned pineapple

salt

chopped fresh coriander, to garnish

method

1 If you are using wooden skewers for this rather than metal ones, place 4 skewers upright in a tall glass of water to soak for 20 minutes so they do not burn under the grill.

2 Dry-roast the cumin, coriander, fennel, mustard, fenugreek and nigella seeds in a hot frying pan over a high heat, stirring them around constantly, until you can smell the aroma of the spices. Immediately tip the spices out of the pan so they do not burn.

3 Put the spices in a spice grinder or mortar, add the chilli powder and salt to taste and grind to a fine powder. Transfer to a non-metallic bowl and stir in the lemon juice.

4 Add the prawns to the bowl and stir them around so they are well coated, then set aside to marinate for 10 minutes. Meanwhile, preheat the grill to high.

5 Thread 3 prawns and 3 pineapple wedges alternately onto each wooden or metal skewer. Grill about 10 cm/4 inches from the heat for 2 minutes on each side, brushing with any leftover marinade, until the prawns turn pink and are cooked through.

6 Serve the prawns and pineapple wedges on the skewers on a plate with plenty of fresh coriander sprinkled over.

prawns in coconut milk with chillies & curry leaves

ingredients

SERVES 4

4 tbsp sunflower or olive oil

1/2 tsp black or brown mustard seeds

1/2 tsp fenugreek seeds

1 large onion, finely chopped

2 tsp garlic purée

2 tsp ginger purée

1–2 fresh green chillies, chopped (deseeded if you like)

1 tbsp ground coriander

1/2 tsp ground turmeric

1/2 tsp chilli powder

1 tsp salt, or to taste

250 ml/9 fl oz canned coconut milk

450 g/1 lb cooked peeled tiger prawns, thawed and drained if frozen

1 tbsp tamarind juice or juice of 1/2 lime

1/2 tsp crushed black pepper

10–12 fresh or dried curry leaves

method

1 Heat 3 tablespoons of the oil in a medium saucepan over a medium–high heat. When hot, but not smoking, add the mustard seeds, followed by the fenugreek seeds and the onion. Cook, stirring frequently, for 5–6 minutes, until the onion is soft but not brown. Add the garlic and ginger purées and the chillies and cook, stirring frequently, for a further 5–6 minutes, until the onion is a light golden colour.

2 Add the coriander, turmeric and chilli powder and cook, stirring, for 1 minute. Add the salt and coconut milk, followed by the prawns and tamarind juice. Bring to a slow simmer and cook, stirring occasionally, for 3–4 minutes.

3 Meanwhile, heat the remaining oil in a very small saucepan over a medium heat. Add the pepper and curry leaves. Turn off the heat and leave to sizzle for 20–25 seconds, then fold the aromatic oil into the prawn mixture. Remove from the heat and serve immediately.

mussels with mustard seeds & shallots

ingredients

SERVES 4

2 kg/4 lb 8 oz live mussels, scrubbed and debearded

3 tbsp vegetable or groundnut oil

$1/2$ tbsp black mustard seeds

8 shallots, chopped

2 garlic cloves, crushed

2 tbsp distilled vinegar

4 small fresh red chillies

85 g/3 oz creamed coconut, dissolved in 300 ml/ 10 fl oz boiling water

10 fresh or 1 tbsp dried curry leaves

$1/2$ tsp ground turmeric

$1/4$–$1/2$ tsp chilli powder

salt

method

1 Discard any mussels with broken shells and any that refuse to close when tapped with a knife. Set aside.

2 Heat the oil in a wok or large frying pan over a medium–high heat. Add the mustard seeds and stir them around for about 1 minute, or until they start to pop.

3 Add the shallots and garlic and cook, stirring frequently, for 3 minutes, or until they start to brown. Stir in the vinegar, whole chillies, dissolved creamed coconut, curry leaves, turmeric, chilli powder and a pinch of salt and bring to the boil, stirring.

4 Reduce the heat to very low. Add the mussels, cover the pan and leave the mussels to simmer, shaking the pan frequently, for 3–4 minutes, or until they are all open. Discard any mussels that remain closed. Ladle the mussels into deep bowls, then taste the broth and add extra salt, if necessary. Spoon over the mussels and serve.

mussels in coconut sauce

ingredients

SERVES 4

1 kg/2 lb 4 oz live mussels, scrubbed and debearded

3 tbsp ghee or vegetable oil

1 onion, finely chopped

1 tsp garlic purée

1 tsp ginger purée

1 tsp ground cumin

1 tsp ground coriander

$1/2$ tsp ground turmeric

pinch of salt

600 ml/1 pint canned coconut milk

chopped fresh coriander, to garnish

method

1 Discard any mussels with broken shells and any that refuse to close when tapped with a knife. Set aside.

2 Heat the ghee in a large heavy-based frying pan. Add the onion and cook over a low heat, stirring occasionally, for 10 minutes, or until golden.

3 Add the garlic and ginger purées and cook, stirring constantly, for 2 minutes. Add the cumin, ground coriander, turmeric and salt and cook, stirring constantly, for a further 2 minutes. Stir in the coconut milk and bring to the boil.

4 Add the mussels, cover and cook for 5 minutes, or until the mussels have opened. Discard any mussels that remain closed. Transfer the mussels, with the coconut sauce, to a large warmed serving dish. Sprinkle with chopped coriander and serve immediately.

vegetables & pulses

Many Indians are vegetarian either through religious belief or as a result of poverty, so the imaginative diversity of dishes based on vegetables and pulses is breathtaking. Indian cooks treat vegetables with great respect – not surprising in a country that boasts 18 different varieties of spinach. The keynote of vegetable dishes is contrasting flavours so hot spices are matched with cooling yogurt or sour tamarind, and savoury greens with sweet nuts or fruit. Virtually all vegetables familiar to western cooks are at home in the Indian kitchen too – onions, potatoes, aubergines, peppers, tomatoes, cauliflower, okra, spinach, peas and green beans – so as well as a huge choice of main-course vegetarian dishes, there is always an ideal side dish to choose.

Pulses, whether dried beans, chickpeas, lentils or split peas, are very nutritious and have a natural affinity with herbs and spices. They may be cooked whole or puréed and made into dhal – virtually every region of India has its own dhal speciality. They can also, of course, be combined with each other and/or vegetables.

With the exception of lentils, pulses need to be soaked in cold water before cooking. However, for your convenience, most of the recipes in this book use canned pulses, which are pre-soaked and cooked and therefore considerably reduce the overall cooking time.

vegetable korma

ingredients

SERVES 4

85 g/3 oz raw cashew nuts

175 ml/6 fl oz boiling water

good pinch of saffron threads,
   pounded

2 tbsp hot milk

1 small cauliflower, divided
   into 1-cm/$1/2$-inch florets

115 g/4 oz green beans, cut
   into 2.5-cm/1-inch lengths

115 g/4 oz carrots, cut into
   2.5-cm/1-inch sticks

4 tbsp sunflower or olive oil

1 large onion, finely chopped

2 tsp ginger purée

1–2 fresh green chillies,
   chopped (deseeded if
   you like)

2 tsp ground coriander

$1/2$ tsp ground turmeric

6 tbsp warm water

400 ml/14 fl oz vegetable
   stock

$1/2$ tsp salt, or to taste

250 g/9 oz new potatoes,
   boiled in their skins and
   cooled, halved

2 tbsp single cream

2 tsp ghee or butter

1 tsp garam masala

$1/4$ tsp grated nutmeg

method

1 Soak the cashew nuts in the boiling water in a heatproof bowl for 20 minutes. Meanwhile, soak the pounded saffron in the hot milk.

2 Blanch the vegetables in a saucepan of boiling salted water, then drain and immediately plunge in cold water. The cauliflower and green beans should each be blanched for 3 minutes, whilst carrots will need 4 minutes.

3 Heat the oil in a medium heavy-based saucepan over a medium heat. Add the onion, ginger purée and chillies and cook, stirring frequently, for 5–6 minutes, until the onion is soft. Add the coriander and turmeric and cook, stirring, for 1 minute. Add half the warm water and cook for 2–3 minutes. Repeat this process, then cook, stirring frequently, for 2–3 minutes, or until the oil separates from the spice paste.

4 Add the stock, saffron and milk mixture and salt, and bring to the boil. Drain the vegetables, add to the saucepan with the potatoes and return to the boil. Reduce the heat to low and simmer for 2–3 minutes.

5 Meanwhile, put the cashew nuts and their soaking water in a food processor and process until well blended. Add to the korma, then stir in the cream. Reduce the heat to very low.

6 Melt the ghee in a small saucepan over a low heat. Add the garam masala and nutmeg and sizzle gently for 20–25 seconds. Fold the spiced butter into the korma. Remove from the heat and serve.

cauliflower, aubergine & green bean korma

ingredients

SERVES 4–6

85 g/3 oz cashew nuts

1^1/$_2$ tbsp garlic and ginger
   paste

200 ml/7 fl oz water

55 g/2 oz ghee or 4 tbsp
   vegetable or groundnut oil

1 large onion, chopped

5 green cardamom pods,
   bruised

1 cinnamon stick,
   broken in half

^{1}/$_4$ tsp ground turmeric

250 ml/9 fl oz double cream

140 g/5 oz new potatoes,
   scrubbed and chopped
   into 1-cm/^{1}/$_2$-inch pieces

140 g/5 oz cauliflower florets

^{1}/$_2$ tsp garam masala

140 g/5 oz aubergine,
   chopped into 2.5-cm/
   1-inch chunks

140 g/5 oz green beans,
   chopped into 2.5-cm/
   1-inch lengths

salt and pepper

chopped fresh mint,
   to garnish

method

1 Heat a large flameproof casserole over a high heat. Add the cashew nuts and stir them around until they start to brown, then immediately tip them out of the casserole.

2 Put the nuts in a spice grinder with the garlic and ginger paste and 1 tablespoon of the water and whizz until a coarse paste forms.

3 Melt half the ghee in the casserole over a medium–high heat. Add the onion and cook for 5–8 minutes, until golden brown.

4 Add the nut paste and stir for 5 minutes. Stir in the cardamom pods, cinnamon stick and turmeric.

5 Add the cream and the remaining water and bring to the boil, stirring. Reduce the heat to very low, cover and simmer for 5 minutes.

6 Add the potatoes, cauliflower and garam masala and simmer, covered, for 5 minutes. Stir in the aubergine and green beans and simmer for a further 5 minutes, or until all the vegetables are tender. Check the sauce occasionally to make sure it isn't sticking, and stir in a little water if needed.

7 Taste and add seasoning, if necessary. Sprinkle with the mint and serve.

cumin-scented aubergine & potato curry

ingredients

SERVES 4

1 large aubergine, about
    350 g/12 oz
225 g/8 oz potatoes, boiled in
    their skins and cooled
3 tbsp sunflower or olive oil
$1/2$ tsp black mustard seeds
$1/2$ tsp nigella seeds
$1/2$ tsp fennel seeds
1 onion, finely chopped
2.5-cm/1-inch piece fresh
    ginger, grated
2 fresh green chillies,
    chopped (deseeded if
    you like)
$1/2$ tsp ground cumin
1 tsp ground coriander
1 tsp ground turmeric
$1/2$ tsp chilli powder
1 tbsp tomato purée
450 ml/15 fl oz warm water
1 tsp salt, or to taste
$1/2$ tsp garam masala
2 tbsp chopped fresh
    coriander leaves
Indian bread, to serve

method

1 Quarter the aubergine lengthways and cut the stem end of each quarter into 5-cm/2-inch pieces. Halve the remaining part of each quarter and cut into the same size as above. Soak the aubergine pieces in cold water.

2 Peel the potatoes and cut into into 5-cm/ 2-inch cubes. Set aside. Heat the oil in a large saucepan over a medium heat. When hot, add the mustard seeds and, as soon as they start popping, add the nigella seeds and fennel seeds.

3 Add the onion, ginger and chillies and cook for 7–8 minutes, until the mixture begins to brown.

4 Add the cumin, coriander, turmeric and chilli powder. Cook for about a minute, then add the tomato purée. Cook for a further minute, pour in the warm water, then add the salt and aubergine. Bring to the boil and cook over a medium heat for 8–10 minutes, stirring frequently to ensure that the aubergine cooks evenly. At the start of cooking, the aubergine will float, but once it soaks up the liquid it will sink quite quickly. As soon as the aubergine sinks, add the potatoes and cook for a further 2–3 minutes, stirring.

5 Stir in the garam masala and chopped coriander and remove from the heat. Serve with Indian bread.

pumpkin curry

ingredients

SERVES 4

150 ml/5 fl oz vegetable oil

2 onions, sliced

$^1/_2$ tsp white cumin seeds

450 g/1 lb pumpkin, cubed

1 tsp amchoor (dried mango powder)

1 tsp finely chopped fresh ginger

1 tsp crushed garlic

1 tsp crushed red chilli

$^1/_2$ tsp salt

300 ml/10 fl oz water

chapatis, to serve

method

1 Heat the oil in a large heavy-based frying pan. Add the onions and cumin seeds and cook, stirring occasionally, for 5–6 minutes, until a light golden brown colour.

2 Add the pumpkin to the frying pan and stir-fry for 3–5 minutes over a low heat.

3 Mix the amchoor, ginger, garlic, chilli and salt together in a bowl. Add to the onion and pumpkin mixture in the pan and stir well.

4 Add the water, cover and cook over a low heat for 10–15 minutes, stirring occasionally. Transfer the curry to serving plates and serve hot with chapatis.

cauliflower & sweet potato curry

ingredients

SERVES 4

4 tbsp ghee or vegetable oil

2 onions, finely chopped

1 tsp panch phoran

1 cauliflower, broken into
small florets

350 g/12 oz sweet potatoes,
diced

2 fresh green chillies,
deseeded and finely
chopped

1 tsp ginger purée

2 tsp paprika

$1^1/_2$ tsp ground cumin

1 tsp ground turmeric

$^1/_2$ tsp chilli powder

3 tomatoes, quartered

225 g/8 oz fresh or frozen
peas

3 tbsp natural yogurt

225 ml/8 fl oz vegetable stock
or water

1 tsp garam masala

salt

fresh coriander sprigs,
to garnish

method

1 Heat the ghee in a large heavy-based frying pan. Add the onions and panch phoran and cook over a low heat, stirring frequently, for 10 minutes, or until the onions are golden. Add the cauliflower, sweet potatoes and chillies and cook, stirring frequently, for 3 minutes.

2 Stir in the ginger purée, paprika, cumin, turmeric and chilli powder and cook, stirring constantly, for 3 minutes. Add the tomatoes and peas and stir in the yogurt and stock. Season with salt to taste, cover and simmer for 20 minutes, or until the vegetables are tender.

3 Sprinkle over the garam masala and transfer to a warmed serving dish. Garnish with coriander sprigs and serve immediately.

mushroom bhaji

ingredients

SERVES 4

280 g/10 oz closed-cup white
    mushrooms
4 tbsp sunflower or olive oil
1 onion, finely chopped
1 fresh green chilli, finely
    chopped (deseeded if
    you like)
2 tsp garlic purée
1 tsp ground cumin
1 tsp ground coriander
$^1/_2$ tsp chilli powder
$^1/_2$ tsp salt, or to taste
1 tbsp tomato purée
3 tbsp water
1 tbsp snipped fresh chives,
    to garnish

method

1 Wipe the mushrooms with damp kitchen paper and thickly slice.

2 Heat the oil in a medium saucepan over a medium heat. Add the onion and chilli and cook, stirring frequently, for 5–6 minutes, until the onion is soft but not brown. Add the garlic purée and cook, stirring, for 2 minutes.

3 Add the cumin, coriander and chilli powder and cook, stirring, for 1 minute. Add the mushrooms, salt and tomato purée and stir until all the ingredients are thoroughly blended.

4 Sprinkle the water evenly over the mushrooms and reduce the heat to low. Cover and cook for 5 minutes, stir, then cook for a further 5 minutes. The sauce should have thickened, but if it appears runny, cook, uncovered, for 3–4 minutes, or until you achieve the desired consistency.

5 Transfer to a serving dish, sprinkle the chives on top and serve immediately.

okra stir-fried with onions

ingredients

SERVES 4

280 g/10 oz okra

1 small red pepper

1 onion

2 tbsp sunflower or olive oil

1 tsp black or brown
mustard seeds

$1/2$ tsp cumin seeds

3 large garlic cloves, lightly
crushed, then chopped

$1/2$ tsp chilli powder

$1/2$ tsp salt, or to taste

$1/2$ tsp garam masala

cooked basmati rice,
to serve

method

1 Scrub each okra gently, rinse well in cold running water, then slice off the hard head. Halve diagonally and set aside.

2 Remove the seeds and core from the red pepper and cut into 4-cm/1$1/2$-inch strips. Halve the onion lengthways and cut into 5 mm/$1/4$ inch thick slices.

3 Heat the oil in a heavy-based frying pan or wok over a medium heat. When hot, but not smoking, add the mustard seeds, followed by the cumin seeds. Remove from the heat and add the garlic. Return to a low heat and cook the garlic gently, stirring, for 1 minute, or until lightly browned.

4 Add the okra, red pepper and onion, increase the heat to medium–high and stir-fry for 2 minutes. Add the chilli powder and salt and stir-fry for a further 3 minutes. Add the garam masala and stir-fry for 1 minute. Remove from the heat and serve immediately with cooked basmati rice.

spiced balti cabbage

ingredients

SERVES 4

2 tbsp vegetable or groundnut
oil

$^1/_2$ tbsp cumin seeds

2 large garlic cloves, crushed

1 large onion, thinly sliced

600 g/1 lb 5 oz Savoy
cabbage, cored and
thinly sliced

150 ml/5 fl oz balti sauce
(see page 66)

$^1/_4$ tsp garam masala

salt

chopped fresh coriander,
to garnish

method

1 Heat the oil in a wok or large frying pan over a medium–high heat. Add the cumin seeds and stir for about 80 seconds, until they start to brown.

2 Immediately stir in the garlic and onion and fry, stirring frequently, for 5–8 minutes, until golden.

3 Add the cabbage to the pan and stir for 2 minutes, or until it starts to wilt. Stir in the balti sauce and bring to the boil, stirring. Reduce the heat a little and simmer for 3–5 minutes, until the cabbage is tender.

4 Stir in the garam masala and add salt to taste. Sprinkle with the fresh coriander and serve.

garlic & chilli-flavoured potatoes with cauliflower

ingredients

SERVES 4

350 g/12 oz new potatoes

1 small cauliflower

2 tbsp sunflower or olive oil

1 tsp black or brown mustard seeds

1 tsp cumin seeds

5 large garlic cloves, lightly crushed, then chopped

1–2 fresh green chillies, finely chopped (deseeded if you like)

$1/2$ tsp ground turmeric

$1/2$ tsp salt, or to taste

2 tbsp chopped fresh coriander leaves

method

1 Cook the potatoes in their skins in a saucepan of boiling water for 20 minutes, or until tender. Drain, then soak in cold water for 30 minutes. Peel them, if you like, then halve or quarter according to their size – they should be only slightly bigger than the size of the cauliflower florets.

2 Meanwhile, divide the cauliflower into about 1-cm/$1/2$-inch florets and blanch in a large saucepan of boiling salted water for 3 minutes. Drain and plunge into iced water to prevent further cooking, then drain again.

3 Heat the oil in a medium saucepan over a medium heat. When hot, but not smoking, add the mustard seeds, then the cumin seeds. Remove from the heat and add the garlic and chillies. Return to a low heat and cook, stirring, until the garlic has a light brown tinge.

4 Stir in the turmeric, followed by the cauliflower and the potatoes. Add the salt, increase the heat slightly and cook, stirring, until the vegetables are well blended with the spices and heated through.

5 Stir in the coriander, remove from the heat and serve immediately.

new potatoes with spiced spinach

ingredients

SERVES 4

350 g/12 oz new potatoes

250 g/9 oz spinach leaves, thawed if frozen

3 tbsp sunflower or olive oil

1 large onion, finely sliced

1 fresh green chilli, finely chopped (deseeded if you like)

2 tsp garlic purée

2 tsp ginger purée

1 tsp ground coriander

$^{1}/_{2}$ tsp ground cumin

$^{1}/_{2}$ tsp chilli powder

$^{1}/_{2}$ tsp ground turmeric

200 g/7 oz canned chopped tomatoes

$^{1}/_{2}$ tsp granulated sugar

1 tsp salt, or to taste

3 tbsp single cream

method

1 Cook the potatoes in their skins in a saucepan of boiling water for 20 minutes, or until tender. Drain, then soak in cold water for 30 minutes. Peel them, if you like, then halve or quarter.

2 Meanwhile, cook the spinach in a saucepan of boiling water for 2 minutes, then drain. Transfer to a food processor and blend to a purée.

3 Heat 2 tablespoons of the oil in a medium saucepan over a medium heat. Add the onion and cook, stirring, for 10–12 minutes, until browned, reducing the heat to low for the last 2–3 minutes. Remove from the heat and remove the excess oil from the onion by pressing it against the side of the saucepan with a wooden spoon. Drain on kitchen paper.

4 Return the pan to the heat, add the remaining oil and heat. Add the chilli and garlic and ginger purées and cook over low heat, stirring, for 2–3 minutes. Add the coriander, cumin, chilli powder and turmeric and cook, stirring, for 1 minute. Add the tomatoes, increase the heat to medium and add the sugar. Cook, stirring, for 5–6 minutes.

5 Add the potatoes, spinach, salt and reserved onion and cook, stirring, for 2–3 minutes. Stir in the cream and cook for 1 minute. Remove from the heat and serve.

peas & paneer in chilli-tomato sauce

ingredients

SERVES 4

4 tbsp sunflower or olive oil

250 g/9 oz paneer, cut into
2.5-cm/1-inch cubes

4 green cardamom pods,
bruised

2 bay leaves

1 onion, finely chopped

2 tsp garlic purée

2 tsp ginger purée

2 tsp ground coriander

$1/2$ tsp ground turmeric

$1/2$–1 tsp chilli powder

150 g/$5^1/2$ oz canned
chopped tomatoes

425 ml/15 fl oz warm water,
plus 2 tbsp

1 tsp salt, or to taste

125 g/$4^1/2$ oz frozen peas

$1/2$ tsp garam masala

2 tbsp single cream

2 tbsp chopped fresh
coriander leaves

method

1 Heat 2 tablespoons of the oil in a medium non-stick saucepan over a medium heat. Add the paneer and cook, stirring frequently, for 3–4 minutes, or until evenly browned. Paneer tends to splatter in hot oil, so be careful. Remove and drain on kitchen paper.

2 Add the remaining oil to the saucepan and reduce the heat to low. Add the cardamom pods and bay leaves and leave to sizzle gently for 20–25 seconds. Add the onion, increase the heat to medium and cook, stirring frequently, for 4–5 minutes, until the onion is soft. Add the garlic and ginger purées and cook, stirring frequently, for a further 3–4 minutes, until the onion is a pale golden colour.

3 Add the ground coriander, turmeric and chilli powder and cook, stirring, for 1 minute. Add the tomatoes and cook, stirring, for 4–5 minutes. Add the 2 tablespoons of warm water and cook, stirring, for 3 minutes, or until the oil separates from the spice paste.

4 Add the 425 ml/15 fl oz of warm water and the salt. Bring to the boil, then reduce the heat to low and simmer, uncovered, for 7–8 minutes.

5 Add the paneer and peas and simmer for 5 minutes. Stir in the garam masala, cream and fresh coriander and remove from the heat. Serve immediately.

chickpeas in coconut milk

ingredients

SERVES 4

275 g/9³/₄ oz potatoes, cut
    into 1-cm/¹/₂-inch cubes
250 ml/9 fl oz hot water
400 g/14 oz canned chickpeas,
    drained and well rinsed
250 ml/9 fl oz canned
    coconut milk
1 tsp salt, or to taste
2 tbsp sunflower or olive oil
4 large garlic cloves, finely
    chopped or crushed
2 tsp ground coriander
¹/₂ tsp ground turmeric
¹/₂–1 tsp chilli powder
juice of ¹/₂ lemon
Indian bread, to serve

method

1 Put the potatoes in a medium saucepan and pour in the hot water. Bring to the boil, then reduce the heat to low and cook, covered, for 6–7 minutes, until the potatoes are al dente. Add the chickpeas and cook, uncovered, for 3–4 minutes, until the potatoes are tender. Add the coconut milk and salt and bring to a slow simmer.

2 Meanwhile, heat the oil in a small saucepan over a low heat. Add the garlic and cook, stirring frequently, until it begins to brown. Add the coriander, turmeric and chilli powder and cook, stirring, for 25–30 seconds.

3 Fold the aromatic oil into the chickpea mixture. Stir in the lemon juice and remove from the heat. Serve immediately with Indian bread.

chickpeas with spiced tomatoes

ingredients

SERVES 4

6 tbsp vegetable or groundnut oil

2 tsp cumin seeds

3 large onions, finely chopped

2 tsp garlic and ginger paste

2 small fresh green chillies, deseeded and thinly sliced

$1^1/_2$ tsp amchoor (dried mango powder)

$1^1/_2$ tsp garam masala

$^3/_4$ tsp ground asafoetida

$^1/_2$ tsp ground turmeric

$^1/_4$–1 tsp chilli powder

3 large, firm tomatoes, about 450 g/1 lb, grated

800 g/1 lb 12 oz canned chickpeas, rinsed and drained

6 tbsp water

300 g/$10^1/_2$ oz fresh spinach leaves, rinsed

$^1/_2$ tsp salt, or to taste

method

1 Heat the oil in a wok or large frying pan over a medium–high heat. Add the cumin seeds and stir around for 30 seconds, or until they brown and crackle, watching carefully because they can burn quickly.

2 Immediately stir in the onions, garlic and ginger paste and chillies and fry, stirring frequently, for 5–8 minutes, until the onions are golden.

3 Stir in the amchoor, garam masala, asafoetida, turmeric and chilli powder. Add the tomatoes to the pan, stir them around and continue frying, stirring frequently, until the sauce blends together and starts to brown slightly.

4 Stir in the chickpeas and water and bring to the boil. Reduce the heat to very low and use a wooden spoon or a potato masher to mash about a quarter of the chickpeas, leaving the remainder whole.

5 Add the spinach to the pan with just the water clinging to the leaves and stir around until it wilts and is cooked. Stir in the salt, then taste and adjust the seasoning, adding more salt if necessary.

spiced black-eyed beans & mushrooms

ingredients

SERVES 4

1 onion, roughly chopped

4 large garlic cloves, roughly chopped

2.5-cm/1-inch piece fresh ginger, roughly chopped

4 tbsp sunflower or olive oil

1 tsp ground cumin

1 tsp ground coriander

$^1/_2$ tsp ground fennel

1 tsp ground turmeric

$^1/_2$–1 tsp chilli powder

175 g/6 oz canned chopped tomatoes

400 g/14 oz canned black-eyed beans, drained and rinsed

115 g/4 oz large flat mushrooms, wiped and cut into bite-sized pieces

$^1/_2$ tsp salt, or to taste

175 ml/6 fl oz warm water

1 tbsp chopped fresh mint

1 tbsp chopped fresh coriander leaves

Indian bread, to serve

method

1 Purée the onion, garlic and ginger in a food processor or blender.

2 Heat the oil in a medium saucepan over a medium heat and add the puréed ingredients. Cook for 4–5 minutes, then add the cumin, ground coriander, ground fennel, turmeric and chilli powder. Stir-fry for about a minute, then add the tomatoes. Cook until the tomatoes are pulpy and the juice has evaporated.

3 Add the black-eyed beans, mushrooms and salt. Stir well and pour in the warm water, bring to the boil, cover the pan and reduce the heat to low. Simmer for 8–10 minutes, stirring halfway through.

4 Stir in the chopped mint and coriander and remove from the heat. Transfer to a serving dish and serve with Indian bread.

lentils with fresh chillies, mint & coriander

ingredients

SERVES 4

85 g/3 oz red split lentils (masoor dhal)

85 g/3 oz skinless split chickpeas (channa dhal)

3 tbsp sunflower or olive oil

1 onion, finely chopped

2–3 fresh green chillies, chopped (deseeded if you like)

2 tsp garlic purée

2 tsp ginger purée

1 tsp ground cumin

600 ml/1 pint warm water

1 tsp salt, or to taste

1 tbsp chopped fresh mint

1 tbsp chopped fresh coriander leaves

55 g/2 oz unsalted butter

1 fresh green chilli and 1 small tomato, deseeded and cut into julienne strips, to garnish

method

1 Wash the lentils and chickpeas together until the water runs clear and leave to soak for 30 minutes.

2 Heat the oil in a medium saucepan, preferably non-stick, over a medium heat and add the onion, chillies and garlic and ginger purées. Stir-fry the mixture until it begins to brown.

3 Drain the lentils and chickpeas and add to the onion mixture together with the cumin. Reduce the heat to low and stir-fry for 2–3 minutes, then pour in the warm water. Bring to the boil, reduce the heat to low, cover and simmer 25–30 minutes.

4 Stir in the salt, mint, fresh coriander and butter. Stir until the butter has melted, then remove from the heat. Serve garnished with the strips of chilli and tomato.

mixed lentils with five-spice seasoning

ingredients

SERVES 4

125 g/4^1/$_2$ oz red split lentils
  (masoor dhal)
125 g/4^1/$_2$ oz skinless split
  mung beans (mung dhal)
900 ml/1^1/$_2$ pints hot water
1 tsp ground turmeric
1 tsp salt, or to taste
1 tbsp lemon juice
2 tbsp sunflower or olive oil
^{1}/$_4$ tsp black mustard seeds
^{1}/$_4$ tsp cumin seeds
^{1}/$_4$ tsp nigella seeds
^{1}/$_4$ tsp fennel seeds
4–5 fenugreek seeds
2–3 dried red chillies
1 small tomato, deseeded
  and cut into strips, and
  fresh coriander sprigs,
  to garnish
Indian bread, to serve

method

1 Mix the lentils and beans together and wash until the water runs clear. Put them into a saucepan with the hot water. Bring to the boil and reduce the heat slightly. Let it boil for 5–6 minutes, and when the foam subsides, add the turmeric, reduce the heat to low, cover and cook for 20 minutes. Add the salt and lemon juice and beat the dhal with a wire whisk. Add a little more hot water if the dhal is too thick.

2 Heat the oil in a small saucepan over a medium heat. When hot, but not smoking, add the mustard seeds. As soon as they begin to pop, reduce the heat to low and add the cumin seeds, nigella seeds, fennel seeds, fenugreek seeds and dried chillies. Let the spices sizzle until the seeds begin to pop and the chillies have blackened. Pour the contents of the saucepan over the lentils, scraping off every bit from the saucepan.

3 Turn off the heat and keep the saucepan covered until you are ready to serve. Transfer to a serving dish and garnish with tomato strips and coriander sprigs. Serve with Indian bread.

tarka dhal

ingredients

SERVES 4

200 g/7 oz red split lentils
(masoor dhal)

850 ml/1¹/₂ pints water

1 tsp salt, or to taste

2 tsp sunflower or olive oil

¹/₂ tsp black or brown
mustard seeds

¹/₂ tsp cumin seeds

4 shallots, finely chopped

2 fresh green chillies,
chopped (deseeded if
you like)

1 tsp ground turmeric

1 tsp ground cumin

1 fresh tomato, chopped

2 tbsp chopped fresh
coriander leaves

method

1 Wash the lentils until the water runs clear and put into a medium saucepan. Add the water and bring to the boil. Reduce the heat to medium and skim off the foam. Cook, uncovered, for 10 minutes. Reduce the heat to low, cover and cook for 45 minutes, stirring occasionally to ensure that the lentils do not stick to the base of the pan as they thicken. Stir in the salt.

2 Meanwhile, heat the oil in a small saucepan over a medium heat. When hot, but not smoking, add the mustard seeds, followed by the cumin seeds. Add the shallots and chillies and cook, stirring, for 2–3 minutes, then add the turmeric and ground cumin. Add the tomato and cook, stirring, for 30 seconds.

3 Fold the shallot mixture into the cooked lentils. Stir in the coriander, remove from the heat and serve immediately.

kitchri

ingredients

SERVES 4–6

225 g/8 oz basmati rice

30 g/1 oz ghee or 2 tbsp
vegetable or groundnut oil

1 large onion, finely chopped

250 g/9 oz red split lentils
(masoor dhal), rinsed

2 tsp garam masala

1¹/₂ tsp salt, or to taste

pinch of ground asafoetida

850 ml/1¹/₂ pints water

2 tbsp chopped fresh
coriander

chapatis and raita, to serve

method

1 Rinse the basmati rice in several changes of water until the water runs clear, then leave to soak for 30 minutes. Drain and set aside until ready to cook.

2 Melt the ghee in a flameproof casserole or large saucepan with a tight-fitting lid over a medium–high heat. Add the onion and fry for 5–8 minutes, stirring frequently, until golden, but not brown.

3 Stir in the rice and lentils along with the garam masala, salt and asafoetida, and stir for 2 minutes. Pour in the water and bring to the boil, stirring.

4 Reduce the heat to as low as possible and cover the pan tightly. Simmer without lifting the lid for 20 minutes, until the grains are tender and the liquid is absorbed. Re-cover the pan, turn off the heat and leave to stand for 5 minutes.

5 Use 2 forks to mix in the coriander and adjust the seasoning, adding more salt if necessary. Serve with chapatis and raita.

egg & lentil curry

ingredients

SERVES 4

3 tbsp ghee or vegetable oil

1 large onion, chopped

2 garlic cloves, chopped

2.5-cm/1-inch piece fresh
    ginger, chopped

$1/2$ tsp minced chilli or chilli
    powder

1 tsp ground coriander

1 tsp ground cumin

1 tsp paprika

85 g/3 oz red split lentils
    (masoor dhal)

450 ml/16 fl oz vegetable
    stock

225 g/8 oz canned chopped
    tomatoes

6 eggs

55 ml/2 fl oz coconut milk

2 tomatoes, cut into wedges

salt

fresh coriander sprigs,
    to garnish

chapatis, to serve

method

1 Melt the ghee in a saucepan, add the onion and cook gently for 3 minutes. Stir in the garlic, ginger, chilli and spices and cook gently, stirring frequently, for 1 minute. Stir in the lentils, stock and tomatoes and bring to the boil. Reduce the heat, cover and simmer, stirring occasionally, for 30 minutes, until the lentils are tender.

2 Meanwhile, place the eggs in a saucepan of cold water and bring to the boil. Reduce the heat and simmer for 10 minutes. Drain and cover immediately with cold water.

3 Stir the coconut milk into the lentil mixture and season well with salt. Process the mixture in a blender or food processor until smooth. Return to the pan and heat through.

4 Shell the hard-boiled eggs and cut into quarters. Divide the hard-boiled egg quarters and tomato wedges between serving plates. Spoon over the hot lentil sauce and garnish with coriander sprigs. Serve hot with chapatis.

snacks & accompaniments

Tasty snacks are a way of life in India and, in the West, will make a delightful change from crisps or salted nuts served with pre-dinner drinks. More substantial traditional treats, such as samosas (deep-fried pastry parcels) and onion bhaijis (crisp onion fritters), also make great starters, unusual lunches and fabulous party fare.

Rice is always served with Indian meals, often just plainly boiled. More elaborate rice dishes with herbs, spices, nuts and other ingredients are served on special occasions. The most popular type of rice is basmati, a fragrant long-grained variety that is grown in the foothills of the Himalayas. If you have time, rinse it in several changes of cold water and soak for 30 minutes before cooking.

Bread is almost as essential to a meal as rice and is prepared daily in Indian homes. Authentic flat bread is surprisingly quick and easy to make, and even the yeast dough for slipper-shaped naan requires little effort and time, apart from allowing it to rise.

A wonderfully contrasting mixture of tastes and textures characterizes an Indian meal and this is further enhanced with savoury chutneys, pickles and relishes. Whether a cooling yogurt-based raita or a hot lime pickle, these flavoursome accompaniments add the final touch of perfection.

vegetable samosas

ingredients

MAKES 12

3 tbsp sunflower or olive oil

$^1/_2$ tsp black mustard seeds

1 tsp cumin seeds

1 tsp fennel seeds

1 onion, finely chopped

2 fresh green chillies, finely
    chopped (deseeded if
    you like)

2 tsp ginger purée

$^1/_2$ tsp ground turmeric

1 tsp ground coriander

1 tsp ground cumin

$^1/_2$ tsp chilli powder

350 g/12 oz boiled potatoes,
    cut into bite-sized pieces

125 g/4$^1/_2$ oz frozen peas,
    thawed

1 tsp salt, or to taste

2 tbsp chopped fresh
    coriander leaves

12 sheets filo pastry, about
    28 x 18 cm/11 x 7 inches

55 g/2 oz butter, melted,
    plus extra for greasing

chutney, to serve

method

1 Heat the oil in a saucepan over a medium heat and add the mustard seeds, followed by the cumin and fennel seeds. Add the onion, chillies and ginger purée and cook, stirring frequently, for 5–6 minutes.

2 Add the ground spices and cook, stirring, for 1 minute. Add the potatoes, peas and salt and stir until the vegetables are thoroughly coated with the spices. Stir in the coriander and remove from the heat. Leave to cool completely.

3 Preheat the oven to 180°C/350°F/Gas Mark 4 and line a baking sheet with baking paper.

4 Place a sheet of filo pastry on a board and brush well with the melted butter. Keep the remaining pastry sheets covered with a moist cloth or clingfilm. Fold the buttered pastry sheet in half lengthways, brush with some more melted butter and fold lengthways again.

5 Place about 1 tablespoon of the vegetable filling on the bottom right-hand corner of the pastry sheet and fold over to form a triangle. Continue folding to the top of the sheet, maintaining the triangular shape. Transfer to the prepared baking sheet and brush with melted butter. Repeat with the remaining sheets of filo pastry and filling.

6 Bake in the preheated oven for 20 minutes, or until browned. Serve hot with chutney.

onion bhajis

ingredients

SERVES 4

150 g/5$^{1}/_{2}$ oz gram flour

1 tsp salt, or to taste

small pinch of bicarbonate
    of soda

25 g/1 oz ground rice

1 tsp fennel seeds

1 tsp cumin seeds

2 fresh green chillies, finely
    chopped (deseeded if
    you like)

2 large onions, about 400 g/
    14 oz, sliced into half-rings
    and separated

15 g/$^{1}/_{2}$ oz fresh coriander,
    including the tender
    stalks, finely chopped

200 ml/7 fl oz water

sunflower or olive oil,
    for deep-frying

tomato or mango chutney,
    to serve

method

1 Sift the gram flour into a large bowl and add the salt, bicarbonate of soda, ground rice and fennel and cumin seeds. Mix together thoroughly, then add the chillies, onions and coriander. Gradually pour in the water and mix until a thick batter is formed and all the other ingredients are thoroughly coated with it.

2 Heat enough oil for deep-frying in a wok, deep saucepan or deep-fat fryer over a medium heat to 180°C/350°F, or until a cube of bread browns in 30 seconds. If the oil is not hot enough, the bhajis will be soggy. Add as many small amounts (about $^{1}/_{2}$ tablespoon) of the batter as will fit in a single layer, without overcrowding. Reduce the heat slightly and cook the bhajis for 8–10 minutes, until golden brown and crisp.

3 Remove and drain on kitchen paper. Keep hot in a low oven while you cook the remaining batter.

4 Serve hot with chutney.

savoury cheese cakes

ingredients

MAKES 8

2 large slices day- or two-day-
old white bread, crusts
removed

225 g/8 oz paneer, halloumi
cheese or firm tofu
(drained weight), grated

3 shallots, finely chopped

1 tsp fennel seeds

$1/2$ tsp cumin seeds

1 tbsp chopped fresh mint
leaves or $1/2$ tsp dried mint

2 tbsp chopped fresh
coriander leaves

1 tsp ginger purée

25g/1 oz flaked almonds,
lightly crushed (optional)

1 fresh green chilli, chopped
(deseeded if you like)

$1/2$ tsp garam masala

$1/2$ tsp chilli powder (optional)

$1/2$ tsp salt, or to taste

1 tbsp lemon juice

1 large egg, beaten

sunflower or vegetable oil,
for shallow-frying

method

1 Soak the bread slices in a bowl of water for 1–2 minutes, then squeeze out all the water and crumble the slices between your palms. Put the bread in a large bowl and add all the remaining ingredients, except the oil. Mix well to form a binding consistency.

2 Divide the mixture in half and shape each half into 4 equal-sized flat cakes 5 mm/ $1/4$ inch thick.

3 Pour oil into a frying pan to a depth of 2.5 cm/ 1 inch and heat over a medium heat. Add the cakes and cook for 5 minutes on each side, or until well browned. Drain on kitchen paper and serve hot.

golden cauliflower pakoras

ingredients

SERVES 4

vegetable or groundnut oil,
    for deep-frying
400 g/14 oz cauliflower florets
chutney, to serve

batter

140 g/5 oz gram flour
2 tsp ground coriander
1 tsp garam masala
1 tsp salt
$1/2$ tsp ground turmeric
pinch of chilli powder
15 g/$1/2$ oz ghee, melted,
    or 1 tbsp vegetable or
    groundnut oil
1 tsp lemon juice
150 ml/5 fl oz cold water
2 tsp nigella seeds

method

1 To make the batter, stir the gram flour, coriander, garam masala, salt, turmeric and chilli powder into a large bowl. Make a well in the centre, add the ghee and lemon juice with 2 tablespoons of the water, and stir together to make a thick batter.

2 Slowly beat in enough of the remaining water with an electric hand-held mixer or a whisk to make a smooth batter about the same thickness as double cream. Stir in the nigella seeds. Cover the bowl and set aside to stand for at least 30 minutes.

3 When you are ready to fry, heat enough oil for deep-frying in a wok, deep-fat fryer or large heavy-based saucepan until it reaches 180°C/350°F, or until a cube of bread browns in 30 seconds. Dip one cauliflower floret at a time into the batter and let any excess batter fall back into the bowl, then drop it into the hot oil. Add a few more dipped florets, without overcrowding the pan, and fry for about 3 minutes, or until golden brown and crisp.

4 Use a slotted spoon to remove the fritters from the oil and drain well on crumpled kitchen paper. Continue frying until all the cauliflower florets and batter have been used. Serve the hot fritters with chutney for dipping.

sweet & spicy nuts

ingredients

MAKES 450 G/1 LB

300 g/10^1/$_2$ oz caster sugar

1 tsp sea salt

2 tbsp mild, medium or hot
   curry powder, to taste

1 tsp ground turmeric

1 tsp ground coriander

pinch of chilli powder

450 g/1 lb mixed whole
   blanched almonds
   and shelled cashew nuts

vegetable or groundnut oil,
   for deep-frying

method

1 Mix the sugar, salt, curry powder, turmeric, coriander and chilli powder together in a large bowl, then set aside.

2 Meanwhile, bring a large saucepan of water to the boil. Add the almonds and cashews and blanch for 1 minute, then tip them into a sieve to drain, and shake off as much of the excess water as possible. Immediately toss the nuts with the sugar and spices.

3 Heat enough oil for deep-frying in a wok, deep-fat fryer or large heavy-based saucepan to 180°C/350°F, or until a cube of bread browns in 30 seconds. Use a slotted spoon to remove the nuts from the spice mixture, leaving the spice mixture behind in the bowl, then drop the nuts into the hot oil. Fry them for 3–4 minutes, stirring occasionally and watching carefully because they can burn quickly, until they turn golden.

4 Remove the nuts from the oil with the slotted spoon and toss them in the remaining spice mixture. Tip the nuts into a sieve and shake off the excess spices, then leave to cool completely and crisp up. Store in an airtight container for up to a week.

bhel poori

ingredients

SERVES 4

300 g/10^1/$_2$ oz new potatoes

200 g/7 oz canned
    chickpeas, rinsed and very
    well drained

100 g/3^1/$_2$ oz sev noodles

55 g/2 oz puffed rice

4 tbsp raisins

2 tbsp chopped fresh
    coriander

1 tbsp fennel seeds, toasted
    and cooled

pooris, crushed
    (see page 192)

salt

chaat masala

1 tbsp coriander seeds

1 tbsp cumin seeds

1 tsp black peppercorns

2 dried red chillies

to serve

natural yogurt

tamarind chutney
    (see page 206)

coriander chutney
    (see page 198)

method

1 Bring a large saucepan of salted water to the boil and cook the potatoes for 12–15 minutes, until tender. Drain and run under cold water to cool, then peel and cut into 5-mm/^{1}/4-inch dice. Cover and chill for at least 30 minutes.

2 Meanwhile, to make the chaat masala, heat a dry frying pan over a high heat. Add the coriander and cumin seeds, peppercorns and chillies and stir around until they give off their aroma. Immediately tip them out of the pan to stop the cooking, watching closely because the cumin seeds burn quickly. Grind the toasted spice mixture in a spice grinder or with a pestle and mortar.

3 Use your hands to toss together the potatoes, chickpeas, sev noodles, puffed rice, raisins, coriander, fennel seeds and crushed pooris. Sprinkle with the chaat masala and toss again.

4 Divide the mixture among small serving bowls or place in one large bowl and drizzle with the yogurt and chutneys to taste. It is best eaten straight away so it doesn't become soggy.

plantain chips

ingredients

SERVES 4

4 ripe plantains

1 tsp mild, medium or hot
curry powder, to taste

vegetable or groundnut oil,
for deep-frying

mango chutney, to serve

method

1 Peel the plantains, then cut crossways into 3-mm/$\frac{1}{8}$-inch slices. Put the slices in a bowl, sprinkle over the curry powder and use your hands to lightly toss together.

2 Heat enough oil for deep-frying in a wok, deep-fat fryer or large heavy-based saucepan to 180°C/350°F, or until a cube of bread browns in 30 seconds. Add as many plantain slices as will fit in the pan without overcrowding and fry for 2 minutes, or until golden.

3 Remove the plantain chips from the pan with a slotted spoon and drain well on crumpled kitchen paper. Serve hot with mango chutney.

spiced basmati rice

ingredients

SERVES 4–6

225 g/8 oz basmati rice

30 g/1 oz ghee or 2 tbsp
vegetable or groundnut oil

5 green cardamom pods,
bruised

5 cloves

$1/2$ cinnamon stick

1 tsp fennel seeds

$1/2$ tsp black mustard seeds

2 bay leaves

450 ml/16 fl oz water

$1^1/2$ tsp salt, or to taste

pepper

method

1 Rinse the basmati rice in several changes of water until the water runs clear, then leave to soak for 30 minutes. Drain and set aside until ready to cook.

2 Melt the ghee in a flameproof casserole or large saucepan with a tight-fitting lid over a medium–high heat. Add the spices and bay leaves and stir for 30 seconds. Stir the rice into the casserole so the grains are coated with ghee. Stir in the water and salt and bring to the boil.

3 Reduce the heat to as low as possible and cover the casserole tightly. Simmer, without lifting the lid, for 8–10 minutes, until the grains are tender and all the liquid is absorbed.

4 Turn off the heat and use 2 forks to fluff up the rice. Adjust the seasoning, adding salt and pepper if necessary. Re-cover the pan and leave to stand for 5 minutes.

mint & coriander rice with toasted pine kernels

ingredients

SERVES 4

good pinch of saffron threads, pounded

2 tbsp hot milk

225 g/8 oz basmati rice

2 tbsp sunflower or olive oil

5-cm/2-inch piece cinnamon stick, broken in half

4 green cardamom pods, bruised

2 star anise

2 bay leaves

450 ml/16 fl oz lukewarm water

3 tbsp fresh coriander leaves, finely chopped

2 tbsp fresh mint leaves, finely chopped, or 1 tsp dried mint

1 tsp salt, or to taste

25 g /1 oz pine kernels

method

1 Soak the pounded saffron threads in the hot milk and set aside until you are ready to use. Wash the rice in several changes of cold water until the water runs clear. Leave to soak in fresh cold water for 20 minutes, then leave to drain in a colander.

2 Heat the oil in a medium heavy-based saucepan over a low heat. Add the cinnamon, cardamom, star anise and bay leaves and leave to sizzle gently for 20–25 seconds. Add the rice and stir well to ensure that the grains are coated with the flavoured oil.

3 Add the water, stir once and bring to the boil. Add the saffron and milk, coriander, mint and salt and boil for 2–3 minutes. Cover tightly, reduce the heat to very low and cook for 7–8 minutes. Turn off the heat and leave to stand, covered, for 7–8 minutes.

4 Meanwhile, preheat a small heavy-based frying pan over a medium heat, add the pine kernels and cook, stirring, until lightly toasted. Transfer to a plate and leave to cool.

5 Add half the toasted pine kernels to the rice and fluff up the rice with a fork. Transfer to a serving dish, garnish with the remaining pine kernels and serve immediately.

lemon-laced basmati rice

ingredients

SERVES 4

225 g/8 oz basmati rice

2 tbsp sunflower or olive oil

$1/2$ tsp black or brown
mustard seeds

10–12 curry leaves,
preferably fresh

25 g/1 oz cashew nuts

$1/4$ tsp ground turmeric

1 tsp salt, or to taste

450 ml/16 fl oz hot water

2 tbsp lemon juice

1 tbsp snipped fresh chives,
to garnish

method

1 Wash the rice in several changes of cold water until the water runs clear. Leave to soak in fresh cold water for 20 minutes, then leave to drain in a colander.

2 Heat the oil in a non-stick saucepan over a medium heat. When hot, but not smoking, add the mustard seeds, followed by the curry leaves and the cashew nuts (in that order).

3 Stir in the turmeric, quickly followed by the rice and salt. Cook, stirring, for 1 minute, then add the hot water and lemon juice. Stir once, bring to the boil and boil for 2 minutes. Cover tightly, reduce the heat to very low and cook for 8 minutes. Turn off the heat and leave to stand, covered, for 6–7 minutes.

4 Fork through the rice and transfer to a serving dish. Garnish with the chives and serve immediately.

fruit & nut pilau

ingredients

SERVES 4–6

225 g/8 oz basmati rice

450 ml/16 fl oz water

$1/2$ tsp saffron threads

1 tsp salt, or to taste

30 g/1 oz ghee or 2 tbsp
vegetable or groundnut oil

55 g/2 oz blanched almonds

1 onion, thinly sliced

1 cinnamon stick, broken in
half

seeds from 4 green
cardamom pods

1 tsp cumin seeds

1 tsp black peppercorns,
lightly crushed

2 bay leaves

3 tbsp finely chopped dried
mango

3 tbsp finely chopped dried
apricots

2 tbsp sultanas

55 g/2 oz pistachio nuts,
chopped

method

1 Rinse the basmati rice in several changes of water until the water runs clear, then leave to soak for 30 minutes. Drain and set aside until ready to cook.

2 Boil the water in a small saucepan. Add the saffron threads and salt, remove from the heat and set aside to infuse.

3 Melt the ghee in a flameproof casserole or large saucepan with a tight-fitting lid over a medium–high heat. Add the almonds and stir them around until golden brown, then immediately use a slotted spoon to scoop them out of the casserole.

4 Add the onion to the casserole and fry, stirring frequently, for 5–8 minutes, until golden, but not brown. Add the spices and bay leaves to the pan and stir them around for about 30 seconds.

5 Add the rice into the casserole and stir until the grains are coated with ghee. Add the saffron-infused water and bring to the boil. Reduce the heat to as low as possible, stir in the dried fruit and cover the casserole tightly. Simmer, without lifting the lid, for 8–10 minutes, until the grains are tender and all the liquid is absorbed.

6 Turn off the heat and use 2 forks to mix the almonds and pistachios into the rice. Adjust the seasoning, adding more salt if necessary. Re-cover the pan and leave to stand for 5 minutes.

spiced basmati pilau

ingredients

SERVES 4

500 g/1 lb 2 oz basmati rice
175 g/6 oz broccoli, trimmed
6 tbsp vegetable oil
2 large onions, chopped
225 g/8 oz mushrooms, sliced
2 garlic cloves, crushed
6 green cardamom pods,
     bruised
6 whole cloves
8 black peppercorns
1 cinnamon stick or piece of
     cassia bark
1 tsp ground turmeric
1.2 litres/2 pints vegetable
     stock or water
55 g/2 oz seedless raisins
55 g/2 oz unsalted pistachios,
     roughly chopped
salt and pepper

method

1 Place the rice in a sieve and wash well under cold running water. Drain. Trim off most of the broccoli stalk and cut the head into small florets, then quarter the stalk lengthways and cut diagonally into 1-cm/$1/2$-inch pieces.

2 Heat the oil in a large saucepan. Add the onions and broccoli stalks and cook over a low heat, stirring frequently, for 3 minutes. Add the mushrooms, rice, garlic and spices and cook for 1 minute, stirring, until the rice is coated in oil.

3 Add the stock and season to taste with salt and pepper. Stir in the broccoli florets and return the mixture to the boil. Cover, reduce the heat and cook over a low heat for 15 minutes without uncovering the pan.

4 Remove the pan from the heat and leave the pilau to stand for 5 minutes without uncovering. Remove the whole spices, add the raisins and pistachios and gently fork through to fluff up the grains. Serve the pilau hot.

chapatis

ingredients

MAKES 16

400 g/14 oz chapati flour
(atta), plus extra for dusting
1 tsp salt
1/2 tsp granulated sugar
2 tbsp sunflower or olive oil
250 ml/9 fl oz lukewarm water

method

1 Mix the chapati flour, salt and sugar together in a large bowl. Add the oil and work well into the flour mixture with your fingertips. Gradually add the water, mixing at the same time. When the dough is formed, transfer to a work surface and knead for 4–5 minutes. The dough is ready when all the excess moisture is absorbed by the flour. Alternatively, mix the dough in a food processor. Wrap the dough in clingfilm and leave to rest for 30 minutes.

2 Divide the dough in half, then cut each half into 8 equal-sized pieces. Form each piece into a ball and flatten into a round cake. Dust each cake lightly in the flour and roll out to a 15-cm/6-inch round. Keep the remaining cakes covered while you are working on one. The chapatis will cook better when freshly rolled out, so roll out and cook one at a time.

3 Preheat a heavy-based cast-iron griddle (tawa) or a large heavy-based frying pan over a medium–high heat. Put a chapati on the griddle and cook for 30 seconds. Using a thin spatula or fish slice, turn over and cook until bubbles begin to appear on the surface. Turn over again. Press the edges down gently with a clean cloth to encourage the chapati to puff up – they will not always puff up, but this doesn't matter. Cook until brown patches appear on the underside. Remove from the pan and keep hot by wrapping in a piece of foil lined with kitchen paper. Repeat with the remaining dough cakes.

chilli-coriander naan

ingredients

MAKES 8

450 g/1 lb plain flour

2 tsp sugar

1 tsp salt

1 tsp baking powder

1 egg

250 ml/9 fl oz milk

2 tbsp sunflower or olive oil,
    plus extra for oiling

2 fresh red chillies, chopped
    (deseeded if you like)

15 g/$\frac{1}{2}$ oz fresh coriander
    leaves, chopped

2 tbsp butter, melted

method

1 Sift the flour, sugar, salt and baking powder together into a large bowl. Whisk the egg and milk together, then gradually add to the flour and mix until a dough is formed.

2 Transfer the dough to a work surface, make a depression in the centre of the dough and add the oil. Knead for 3–4 minutes, until you have a smooth and pliable dough. Wrap the dough in clingfilm and leave to rest for 1 hour.

3 Divide the dough into 8 equal-sized pieces, form each piece into a ball and flatten into a thick cake. Cover the dough cakes with clingfilm and leave to rest for 10–15 minutes.

4 Preheat the grill to high, line a grill pan with a piece of foil and brush with oil.

5 Roll each flattened cake into a 12.5-cm/5-inch round and pull the lower end gently. Carefully roll out again, maintaining the teardrop shape, to about 23 cm/9 inches in diameter.

6 Mix the chillies and coriander together, then spread on the surface of the naans. Press gently so that the mixture sticks to the dough. Transfer a naan to the prepared grill pan and cook for 1 minute, or until slightly puffed and brown patches appear on the surface. Turn over and cook the other side for 45–50 seconds, until lightly browned. Remove from the grill and brush with the melted butter. Wrap in a tea towel while you cook the remaining naans.

pooris

ingredients

MAKES 12

225 g/8 oz wholemeal flour,
  sifted, plus extra for
  dusting
$1/2$ teaspoon salt
30 g/1 oz ghee, melted
100–150 ml/$3^1/2$–5 fl oz water
vegetable or groundnut oil,
  for deep-frying

method

1 Put the flour and salt into a bowl and drizzle the ghee over the surface. Gradually stir in the water until a stiff dough forms.

2 Turn out the dough onto a lightly floured surface and knead for 10 minutes, or until it is smooth and elastic. Shape the dough into a ball and place it in a clean bowl, then cover with a damp tea towel and leave to rest for 20 minutes.

3 Divide the dough into 12 equal-sized pieces and roll each into a ball. Working with one ball of dough at a time, flatten the dough between your palms, then thinly roll it out on a lightly floured work surface into a 13-cm/5-inch round. Continue until all the dough balls are rolled out. Alternatively, to make mini pooris, thinly roll out the dough on a lightly floured work surface, then use a 4-cm/$1^1/2$-inch biscuit cutter to stamp out smaller rounds.

4 Heat at least 7.5 cm/3 inches oil in a wok, deep-fat fryer or large frying pan until it reaches 180°C/350°F, or until a cube of bread browns in 30 seconds. Drop one poori into the hot fat and fry for about 10 seconds, or until it puffs up. Use 2 large spoons to flip the poori over and spoon some hot oil over the top.

5 Use the 2 spoons to lift the poori from the oil and let any excess oil drip back into the pan. Drain the poori on crumpled kitchen paper and serve immediately. Continue until all the pooris are fried, making sure the oil returns to the correct temperature before you add another poori.

cucumber raita

ingredients

SERVES 4–5

1 small cucumber

175 g/6 oz whole milk natural
yogurt

$1/4$ tsp granulated sugar

$1/4$ tsp salt

1 tsp cumin seeds

10–12 black peppercorns

$1/4$ tsp paprika

method

1 Peel the cucumber and scoop out the seeds. Cut the flesh into bite-sized pieces and set aside.

2 Put the yogurt in a bowl and beat with a fork until smooth. Add the sugar and salt and mix well.

3 Preheat a small heavy-based saucepan over a medium–high heat. When the pan is hot, turn off the heat and add the cumin seeds and peppercorns. Stir around for 40–50 seconds, until they release their aroma. Remove from the pan and leave to cool for 5 minutes, then crush in a mortar with a pestle or on a hard surface with a rolling pin.

4 Reserve $1/4$ teaspoon of this mixture and stir the remainder into the yogurt. Add the cucumber and stir to mix. Transfer the raita to a serving dish and sprinkle with the reserved toasted spices and the paprika.

mint & spinach chutney

ingredients

SERVES 4–6

55 g/2 oz tender fresh
   spinach leaves
3 tbsp fresh mint leaves
2 tbsp chopped fresh
   coriander leaves
1 small red onion, roughly
   chopped
1 small garlic clove, chopped
1 fresh green chilli, chopped
   (deseeded if you like)
$2^1/_2$ tsp granulated sugar
1 tbsp tamarind juice or juice
   of $^1/_2$ lemon

method

1 Put all the ingredients in a blender or food processor and blend until smooth, adding a little water to enable the blades to move, if necessary.

2 Transfer to a serving bowl, cover and chill in the refrigerator for at least 30 minutes before serving.

coriander chutney

ingredients

MAKES 225 G/8 OZ

1½ tbsp lemon juice

1½ tbsp water

85 g/3 oz fresh coriander
   leaves and stems,
   roughly chopped

2 tbsp chopped fresh coconut

1 small shallot, very finely
   chopped

5-mm/¼-inch piece fresh
   ginger, chopped

1 fresh green chilli, deseeded
   and chopped

½ tsp sugar

½ tsp salt

pinch of pepper

method

1 Put the lemon juice and water in a small food processor, add half the coriander and whizz until it is blended and a slushy paste forms. Gradually add the remaining coriander and whizz until it is all blended, scraping down the sides of the processor, if necessary. If you don't have a processor that will cope with this small amount, use a pestle and mortar, adding the coriander in small amounts.

2 Add the remaining ingredients and continue whizzing until they are all finely chopped and blended. Taste and adjust any of the seasonings, if you like. Transfer to a non-metallic bowl, cover and chill for up to 3 days before serving.

onion & tomato salad

ingredients

SERVES 4

3 tomatoes, deseeded and
   chopped

1 large onion, finely chopped

3 tbsp chopped fresh
   coriander, plus extra to
   garnish

1–2 fresh green chillies,
   deseeded and very finely
   sliced

2 tbsp lemon juice, or to taste

1 tsp salt, or to taste

pinch of sugar

pepper

method

1 Put the tomatoes, onion, coriander and chillies in a bowl. Add the lemon juice, salt, sugar and pepper to taste then gently toss all together. Cover and chill for at least 1 hour.

2 Just before serving, gently toss the salad again. Add extra lemon juice or salt and pepper to taste. Spoon into a serving bowl and sprinkle with fresh coriander.

coconut sambal

ingredients

MAKES 140 G/5 OZ

$1/2$ fresh coconut or 125 g/
    $41/2$ oz desiccated coconut
2 fresh green chillies,
    chopped (deseeded if
    you like)
2.5-cm/1-inch piece fresh
    ginger, peeled and finely
    chopped
4 tbsp chopped fresh coriander
2 tbsp lemon juice, or to taste
2 shallots, very finely chopped

method

1 If you are using a whole coconut, use a hammer and nail to punch a hole in the 'eye' of the coconut, then pour out the water from the inside and reserve. Use the hammer to break the coconut in half, then peel half and chop.

2 Put the coconut and chillies in a food processor and process for about 30 seconds, until finely chopped. Add the ginger, coriander and lemon juice and process again.

3 If the mixture seems too dry, stir in about 1 tablespoon of the reserved coconut water or water. Stir in the shallots and serve immediately, or cover and chill until required.

mango chutney

ingredients

MAKES 250 G/9 OZ

1 large mango, about 400 g/
    14 oz, peeled, stoned and
    finely chopped

2 tbsp lime juice

1 tbsp vegetable or
    groundnut oil

2 shallots, finely chopped

1 garlic clove, finely chopped

2 fresh green chillies,
    deseeded and finely sliced

1 tsp black mustard seeds

1 tsp coriander seeds

5 tbsp palm sugar or soft light
    brown sugar

5 tbsp white wine vinegar

1 tsp salt

pinch of ground ginger

method

1 Put the mango in a non-metallic bowl with the lime juice and set aside.

2 Heat the oil in a large frying pan or saucepan over a medium–high heat. Add the shallots and cook for 3 minutes. Add the garlic and chillies and stir for a further 2 minutes, or until the shallots are soft but not brown. Add the mustard seeds and coriander seeds and then stir around.

3 Add the mango to the pan with the palm sugar, vinegar, salt and ground ginger and stir around. Reduce the heat to its lowest setting and simmer for 10 minutes, until the liquid thickens and the mango becomes sticky.

4 Remove from the heat and leave to cool completely. Transfer to an airtight container, cover and chill for 3 days before using.

tamarind chutney

ingredients

MAKES 250 G/9 OZ

100 g/3^1/$_2$ oz tamarind pulp, chopped

450 ml/16 fl oz water

^{1}/$_2$ fresh bird's eye chilli, or to taste, deseeded and chopped

55 g/2 oz soft light brown sugar, or to taste

^{1}/$_2$ tsp salt, or to taste

method

1 Put the tamarind and water in a heavy-based saucepan over a high heat and bring to the boil. Reduce the heat to the lowest setting and simmer for 25 minutes, stirring occasionally to break up the tamarind pulp, or until tender.

2 Tip the tamarind pulp into a sieve and use a wooden spoon to push the pulp into the rinsed-out pan.

3 Stir in the chilli, sugar and salt and continue simmering for a further 10 minutes, or until the desired consistency is reached. Leave to cool slightly, then stir in extra sugar or salt to taste.

4 Leave to cool completely, then cover tightly and chill for up to 3 days, or freeze.

lime pickle

ingredients

MAKES 225 G/8 OZ

12 limes, halved and deseeded

115 g/4 oz salt

70 g/2$^{1}/_{2}$ oz chilli powder

25 g/1 oz mustard powder

25 g/1 oz ground fenugreek

1 tbsp ground turmeric

300 ml/10 fl oz mustard oil

15 g/$^{1}/_{2}$ oz yellow mustard
    seeds, crushed

$^{1}/_{2}$ tsp asafoetida

method

1 Cut each lime half into 4 pieces and pack them into a large sterilized jar, sprinkling over the salt at the same time. Cover and leave to stand in a warm place for 10–14 days, or until the limes have turned brown and softened.

2 Mix the chilli powder, mustard powder, fenugreek and turmeric together in a small bowl and add to the jar of limes. Stir to mix, then re-cover and leave to stand for 2 days.

3 Transfer the lime mixture to a heatproof bowl. Heat the mustard oil in a heavy-based frying pan. Add the mustard seeds and asafoetida to the pan and cook, stirring constantly, until the oil is very hot and just beginning to smoke.

4 Pour the oil and spices over the limes and mix well. Cover and leave to cool. When cool, pack into a sterilized jar, seal and store in a sunny place for 1 week before serving.

desserts & drinks

Most of us would agree that there can be little more delicious after a hot, spicy main course than a palate-cleansing fruit-based dessert or refreshing iced sweet. Indian-style ice cream, especially with a tropical flavour, is a must-try treat. It's worth noting, too, that it is easier to make at home than western-style ice cream. Indian cooks are also aware that milk has a cooling effect and use it as the basis for a number of popular desserts, from rich rice pudding to halva, an intensely flavoured, fudge-like sweetmeat. Indian desserts are perfect for those with a sweet tooth and are special enough to serve to guests at the end of any meal, whether Indian or western.

Tea has been grown in India since the first half of the nineteenth century. It remains a favourite beverage and is served in a variety of ways, including flavoured with a mix of spices. It is not the only popular drink, however, and is rivalled by the yogurt-based lassi. Sweet and savoury versions are sold at roadside stalls, served in restaurants and made at home to refresh, cool and, it is thought, aid digestion. Finally, we include recipes for cooling citrus-based cordials – the perfect thirst-quenchers at the end of a long, hot summer's day.

mango kulfi

ingredients

SERVES 6–8

375 g/13 oz canned
   evaporated milk
300 ml/10 fl oz single cream
25 g/1 oz ground almonds
115–140 g/4–5 oz granulated
   sugar
450 g/1 lb mango purée
1 tsp freshly ground
   cardamom seeds
25 g/1 oz shelled unsalted
   pistachio nuts, to decorate

method

1 Pour the evaporated milk and cream into a heavy-based saucepan and stir to mix. Put over a medium heat. Mix the ground almonds and sugar together, then add to the milk mixture. Cook, stirring, for 6–8 minutes, until the mixture thickens slightly.

2 Remove from the heat and leave the mixture to cool completely, stirring from time to time to prevent a skin forming. When completely cold, stir in the mango purée and ground cardamom.

3 Meanwhile, preheat a small saucepan over a medium heat, add the pistachio nuts and toast for 2–3 minutes. Leave to cool, then lightly crush. Store in an airtight container until required.

4 Kulfi is set in traditional conical-shaped plastic or steel moulds, which you can buy from Asian stores, but you can use decorative individual jelly moulds or ice lolly moulds instead. Fill the containers of your choice with the kulfi mixture and freeze for 5–6 hours. Transfer the kulfi to the refrigerator for 40 minutes, then invert onto serving dishes. Serve sprinkled with the crushed pistachio nuts to decorate.

indian rice dessert

ingredients

SERVES 4

good pinch of saffron threads, pounded

2 tbsp hot milk

40 g/1^1/$_2$ oz ghee or unsalted butter

55 g/2 oz ground rice

25 g/1 oz flaked almonds

25 g/1 oz seedless raisins

600 ml/1 pint full-fat milk

450 ml/16 fl oz evaporated milk

55 g/2 oz caster sugar

12 ready-to-eat dried apricots, sliced

1 tsp freshly ground cardamom seeds

^{1}/$_2$ tsp freshly grated nutmeg

2 tbsp rosewater

to decorate

25 g/1 oz walnut pieces

15 g/^{1}/$_2$ oz shelled unsalted pistachio nuts

method

1 Place the pounded saffron in the hot milk and leave to soak until needed.

2 Reserve 2 teaspoons of the ghee and melt the remainder in a heavy-based saucepan over a low heat. Add the ground rice, almonds and raisins and cook, stirring, for 2 minutes. Add the full-fat milk, increase the heat to medium and cook, stirring, until it begins to bubble gently. Reduce the heat to low and cook, stirring frequently, for 10–12 minutes, to prevent the mixture from sticking to the bottom of the pan.

3 Add the evaporated milk, sugar and apricots, reserving a few slices to decorate. Cook, stirring, until the mixture thickens to the consistency of a pouring custard.

4 Add the reserved saffron and milk mixture, the cardamom, nutmeg and rosewater, stir to distribute well and remove from the heat. Leave to cool, then cover and chill in the refrigerator for at least 2 hours.

5 Melt the reserved ghee in a small saucepan over a low heat. Add the walnuts and cook, stirring, until they brown a little. Remove and drain on kitchen paper. Brown the pistachio nuts in the saucepan, remove and drain on kitchen paper. Leave the pistachio nuts to cool, then lightly crush.

6 Serve the dessert decorated with the fried nuts and the reserved apricot slices.

sago & coconut pudding

ingredients

SERVES 4

1/2 fresh coconut

225 ml/8 fl oz water

850 ml/1 1/2 pints milk

85 g/3 oz caster sugar

25 g/1 oz raisins

55 g/2 oz sago

seeds from 6–8 green
    cardamom pods

25 g/1 oz flaked almonds,
    for sprinkling

method

1 To prepare the coconut milk, remove the flesh from the coconut half-shell and grate it. Place in a food processor or blender, add the water and process until smooth. Strain through a sieve into a jug, pressing down on the coconut with the back of a wooden spoon. Discard the contents of the sieve and reserve the coconut milk.

2 Bring the 850 ml/1 1/2 pints milk to the boil in a large heavy-based saucepan and continue to boil until it has reduced to 600 ml/1 pint. Reduce the heat, add the sugar and stir until dissolved. Stir in the raisins and sago. Simmer gently for 6–8 minutes, or until the sago is cooked.

3 Remove the saucepan from the heat and stir in the coconut milk and cardamom seeds, then pour into individual serving dishes. Sprinkle with the almonds and leave to cool before serving.

almond sherbet

ingredients

SERVES 2

225 g/8 oz whole almonds

2 tbsp sugar

300 ml/10 fl oz milk

300 ml/10 fl oz water

method

1 Soak the almonds in a large bowl of water for at least 3 hours, or preferably overnight.

2 Using a sharp knife, chop the almonds into small pieces. Grind to a fine paste in a food processor or with a mortar and pestle.

3 Add the sugar to the almond paste and grind again to make a fine paste. Add the milk and water and mix well (in a blender if you have one).

4 Transfer the almond sherbet to a large serving dish. Leave to chill in the refrigerator for 30 minutes. Stir the almond sherbet just before serving.

almond & pistachio dessert

ingredients

SERVES 2

75 g/2³/₄ oz unsalted butter

200 g/7 oz ground almonds

200 g/7 oz sugar

150 ml/5 fl oz single cream

8 almonds, chopped

10 pistachio nuts, chopped

method

1 Melt the butter in a heavy-based saucepan, preferably non-stick, stirring well. Add the ground almonds, sugar and cream, stirring well. Reduce the heat and stir constantly for 10–12 minutes, scraping the base of the saucepan.

2 Increase the heat until the mixture turns a little darker in colour.

3 Transfer the almond mixture to a large, shallow serving dish and smooth the top with the back of a spoon.

4 Decorate the top of the dessert with the chopped almonds and pistachio nuts. Leave to set for 1 hour, then cut into diamond shapes and serve cold.

carrot halva

ingredients

SERVES 4–6

55 g/2 oz ghee or unsalted
butter
2.5-cm/1-inch piece
cinnamon stick, halved
25 g/1 oz flaked almonds
25 g/1 oz cashew nuts
25 g /1 oz seedless raisins
450 g/1 lb grated carrots
600 ml/1 pint full-fat milk
125 g/4^{1}/2 oz caster sugar
^{1}/2 tsp freshly ground
cardamom seeds
^{1}/2 tsp freshly grated nutmeg
50 ml/2 fl oz double cream
2 tbsp rosewater
vanilla ice cream or whipped
double cream, to serve

method

1 Melt the ghee in a heavy-based saucepan over a low heat. Add the cinnamon stick and leave to sizzle gently for 25–30 seconds. Add the almonds and cashew nuts and cook, stirring, until lightly browned. Remove about a dessertspoon of the nuts and reserve.

2 Add the raisins, carrots, milk and sugar to the saucepan, increase the heat to medium and bring the milk to boiling point. Continue to cook over a low–medium heat for 15–20 minutes, until the milk evaporates completely, stirring frequently, and scraping and blending in any thickened milk that sticks to the side of the saucepan. Don't allow any milk that is stuck to the side to brown or burn, as this will give the dessert an unpleasant flavour.

3 Stir in the cardamom, nutmeg, cream and rosewater. Remove from the heat and leave to cool slightly, then serve topped with a scoop of vanilla ice cream or whipped double cream. Sprinkle over the reserved nuts to decorate.

shrikhand with pomegranate

ingredients

SERVES 4

1 litre/1³/₄ pints natural yogurt

¹/₄ tsp saffron threads

2 tbsp milk

55 g/2 oz caster sugar, or to taste

seeds from 2 green cardamom pods

2 pomegranates, or other exotic fruit

method

1 Line a sieve set over a bowl with a piece of muslin large enough to hang over the edge. Add the yogurt, then tie the corners of the muslin into a tight knot and tie them to a tap. Leave the bundle to hang over the sink for 4 hours, or until all the excess moisture drips away.

2 Put the saffron threads in a dry saucepan over a high heat and 'toast', stirring frequently, until you can smell the aroma. Immediately tip them out of the pan. Put the milk in the pan, return the saffron threads and warm just until bubbles appear around the edge, then set aside and leave to infuse.

3 When the yogurt is thick and creamy, put it in a bowl and stir in the sugar, cardamom seeds and saffron mixture and beat until smooth. Taste and add extra sugar, if desired. Cover and chill for at least 1 hour, until well chilled.

4 Meanwhile, to prepare the pomegranate seeds, cut the fruit in half and use a small teaspoon or your fingers to scoop out the seeds.

5 To serve, spoon the yogurt into individual bowls or plates and add the pomegranate seeds.

ginger ice cream with date & tamarind sauce

ingredients

SERVES 4–5

ice cream

1-litre/1³/₄-pint carton vanilla
   ice cream

2 tsp ground ginger

200 g/7 oz chopped
   crystallized ginger, to serve

tamarind sauce

55 g/2 oz seedless raisins

85 g/3 oz stoned dried dates

250 ml/9 fl oz boiling water

2 rounded tsp tamarind
   concentrate or 3 tbsp
   tamarind juice

25 g/1 oz molasses sugar

method

1 Leave the ice cream at room temperature for 35–40 minutes to soften, then transfer to a bowl. Add the ground ginger and beat well. Return to the carton and freeze for 3–4 hours.

2 Meanwhile, to make the sauce, put the raisins and dates in a heatproof bowl, pour over the boiling water and leave to soak for 15–20 minutes. Transfer to a blender or food processor, add the tamarind and sugar and blend to a smooth purée. Transfer to a non-metallic bowl and leave to cool.

3 Put scoops of the ice cream into serving dishes and drizzle over the sauce. Arrange about 1 dessertspoon of crystallized ginger on top of each dessert and serve immediately. Serve any extra sauce separately.

spiced fruit salad

ingredients

SERVES 4

finely grated rind and juice
   of 1 lime
450 g/1 lb fresh fruit, such as
   bananas, guavas, oranges,
   kumquats, mangoes,
   melons and pineapple
yogurt, to serve

spiced syrup

250 g/9 oz caster sugar
150 ml/5 fl oz water
1 vanilla pod, sliced
   lengthways
1 cinnamon stick, broken in
   half
$1/2$ tsp fennel seeds
$1/2$ tsp black peppercorns,
   lightly crushed
$1/2$ tsp cumin seeds

method

1 Begin by making the spiced syrup. Put the sugar, half the water, the vanilla pod, cinnamon stick, fennel seeds, peppercorns and cumin seeds into a small, heavy-based saucepan over a medium–high heat. Slowly bring to the boil, stirring to dissolve the sugar. As soon as the sugar boils, stop stirring and leave the syrup to bubble until it turns a golden brown.

2 Stand back from the pan and stir in the remaining water: the syrup will splash and splatter. Stir again to dissolve any caramel, then remove the pan from the heat and leave the syrup to cool slightly.

3 Meanwhile, put the lime rind and juice in a large heatproof bowl. Prepare and cut each fruit as required and add it to the bowl. If you are using bananas, toss them immediately in the lime juice to prevent discoloration.

4 Pour in the syrup and leave the fruit and syrup to cool completely, then cover the bowl and chill for at least 1 hour before serving with thick, creamy yogurt.

salt lassi

ingredients

SERVES 4–6

700 ml/1^1/$_4$ pints natural
   yogurt

^{1}/$_2$ tsp salt

^{1}/$_4$ tsp sugar

250 ml/9 fl oz cold water

ice cubes

ground cumin and fresh mint
   sprigs, to decorate

method

1 Beat the yogurt, salt and sugar together in a jug or bowl, then add the water and whisk until frothy.

2 Fill 4 or 6 glasses with ice cubes and pour over the yogurt mixture. Lightly dust the top of each glass with ground cumin and decorate with mint sprigs.

mango lassi

ingredients

SERVES 4–6

1 large mango, about 300 g/
 10$\frac{1}{2}$ oz, peeled, stoned
 and roughly chopped

700 ml/1$\frac{1}{4}$ pints natural
 yogurt

250 ml/9 fl oz cold water

about 2 tbsp caster sugar,
 or to taste

fresh lime juice, to taste

ice cubes

ground ginger, to decorate
 (optional)

method

1 Put the mango flesh in a food processor or blender with the yogurt and whizz until smooth. Add the water and whizz again to blend.

2 The amount of sugar you will add depends on how sweet the mango is. Taste and stir in sugar to taste, then stir in the lime juice.

3 Fill 4 or 6 glasses with ice cubes and pour over the mango mixture. Lightly dust the top of each glass with ground ginger, if you like.

masala tea

ingredients

SERVES 4–6

1 litre/1³/₄ pints water

2.5-cm/1-inch piece fresh
ginger, roughly chopped

1 cinnamon stick

3 green cardamom pods,
bruised

3 cloves

1¹/₂ tbsp Assam tea leaves

sugar and milk, to taste

method

1 Pour the water into a heavy-based saucepan over a medium–high heat. Add the ginger, cinnamon, cardamom and cloves and bring to the boil. Reduce the heat and simmer for 10 minutes.

2 Put the tea leaves in a teapot and pour over the water and spices. Stir and leave to infuse for 5 minutes.

3 Strain the tea into teacups and add sugar and milk to taste.

ginger cordial

ingredients

SERVES 4–6

70 g/2¹/₂ oz fresh ginger, very
    finely chopped

¹/₂ tbsp finely grated lemon
    rind

1.2 litres/2 pints boiling water

2 tbsp fresh lemon juice,
    or to taste

4 tbsp caster sugar,
    or to taste

lemon slices and mint sprigs,
    to decorate

method

1 Put the ginger in a heatproof bowl with the lemon rind. Pour over the boiling water, stir and leave to steep overnight.

2 Strain the liquid into a large jug. Stir in the lemon juice and sugar, stirring until the sugar dissolves. Taste and add extra lemon juice and sugar, if you like. Decorate with lemon slices and mint sprigs and serve.

lime cooler

ingredients

SERVES 4

140 g/5 oz caster sugar

5 tbsp freshly squeezed lime juice

1 tsp finely chopped fresh mint, plus extra sprigs to decorate

1 litre/1¾ pints water

crushed ice, to serve

method

1 Place the sugar, lime juice and chopped mint in a large bowl and stir in the water until the sugar has dissolved.

2 Cover the bowl with clingfilm and chill in the refrigerator for 3–4 hours.

3 Strain the mixture through a sieve into a jug, discarding the contents of the sieve. Fill tall glasses with crushed ice and pour in the lime mixture through a sieve. Decorate with mint sprigs and serve immediately.